Alexander Unleashed

In gratitude we would like you to have our companion to *Alexander Unleashed* **completely for free**!

The Alexander Unleashed Companion is an illustrated, full-color collection of **the 55 most important facts** about Alexander the Great's life and accomplishments. It distills the must-know info from *Alexander Unleashed* into an engaging and lightning-quick primer. Get yourself **everything you need** to contextualize Alexander's life in the broad sweep of history.

Scan the QR code to **claim your free downloadable gift** of *The Alexander Unleashed Companion* now!

Alexander Unleashed

A Biography and Military History of the Great Macedonian Who Conquered the Ancient World

Aeon History

uxori liberisque

et

fratri parentibusque

Also by Aeon History

Golden Laurels, Silver Seas: A Concise Survey of Greek History from the Bronze Age to the End of the Hellenistic Period

The Wolves of Mars: An Introductory History of Rome from the Rise of the Monarchy to the Fall of the Western Empire

A Concise History of the Jews: The People Who Wrestled with God, Ghettos, and Genocide to Achieve Modern Statehood

The Introduction to Greek and Roman History Series: Golden Laurels, Silver Seas + The Wolves of Mars – Greek and Roman History from the Bronze Age to the Fall of the Western Roman Empire

Napoleon Unleashed: A History of the Revolutionary, Emperor, and Military Genius who Reshaped Europe and Defined Modern Leadership

and

Grant Unleashed: A Biography of Ulysses S. Grant— The Union General and U.S. President Who Won the American Civil War and Saved the United States

Scan the code to see our full list!

Contents

Introduction

Alexander III of Macedon cuts a dashing figure. A young man, barely out of his teens, thrust into power. Handsome, athletic, and a visionary with a thirst for glory. His ambition knew no bounds, or so it would seem. His untimely death at 32 keeps him ever young, both in artistic depictions and our speculations of what might have been. He marched his armies across vast continents, defying the limits of the known world.

Yet behind the veil of conquest and legend, you find a complex human story filled with triumph, tragedy, and the timeless pursuit of immortality. Alexander's legacy echoes through the ages, shaping civilizations and igniting future generations' imaginations. However, within the grandeur of his accomplishments lies an often-forgotten truth—a narrative of ambition so profound that it reshaped the fabric of history.

Alexander Unleashed strives to make the distant past feel relevant and accessible, showing how the triumphs and tribulations of Alexander the Great resonate with the contemporary challenges and aspirations we face today. By shining a light on human experiences and universal themes that transcend time, we invite you to forge a personal connection with the past, enriching your understanding of yourself and the world around you.

It's important to recognize the complexity of ancient military campaigns and political dynamics. While they may seem overwhelming at first glance, this book aims to simplify these concepts without sacrificing their scope. Through clear explanations and concise analyses, you'll have a straightforward guide through the labyrinth of ancient warfare and diplomacy.

This book is meant to serve as an accessible, comprehensive, and engaging guide to the life and legacy of Alexander the Great. Here, you will find a story that covers the essential aspects of Alexander's life, from his conquests and achievements to his relationships with friends and foes. To offer the reader a chance to deepen their knowledge further than this short volume allows, we've included over 90 references. Most are freely accessible on the internet – none require a specialist degree to comprehend. Alexander was truly larger than life, and over 2,300 years has given rise to many great works of scholarship touching on Alexander and his world.

Finally, this book aims to inspire and facilitate personal growth by examining Alexander's leadership, strategy, and personal journey. His story offers valuable lessons applicable to contemporary life, inspiring us to reflect on our aspirations and potential. With Alexander's achievements in mind, you're encouraged to cultivate resilience, ambition, and vision, and allowing pursue your own path to greatness.

Chapter 1: The World Before Alexander

When you think of Ancient Greece today, you may imagine a realm of timeless beauty and profound intellectual and artistic achievements. In Athens, the Parthenon rose majestically above the city, a symbol of the city-state's power. The southern city-state of Sparta stood as a testament to discipline and military mastery. Corinth thrived as the center for commerce and trade, welcoming ships from across the Mediterranean to its busy ports.

To the north, Macedonia offered a contrasting landscape, with grand palaces and fortifications serving as centers for political and cultural exchange. Far removed from the pursuit of democratic and philosophical ideals of the southern city-states, the Macedonian people forged a distinct identity aided by strong monarchies and martial tradition. Tracing their lineage back to the legendary hero Heracles, the northern realm was destined to reshape the course of history and usher in an era of Macedonian dominance.

The State of the Ancient Greek World

The history of Ancient Greece is marked by intense rivalry between the city-states and other regions, interspersed with short-lived alliances and cooperation, especially when facing external threats. These alliances would fall away as soon as the threat was neutralized, and the city-states would revert to their internal conflicts and power struggles.

The Persian Wars of the 5th century B.C.E. are a prime example of how deep-set differences were cast aside, creating a unified Greek front in the face of the Persian threat. Spanning 499 B.C.E. to 449 B.C.E., the Persian Wars saw a (somewhat) united Greece, known as the Hellenic League, take on the mighty Persian Empire ruled by King Darius I, and later King Xerxes I. The Persians aimed to expand their dominion into mainland Greece, seeing the independent city-states as easy targets for conquest.

The conflict began in 499 B.C.E. when the Greek city-states in Asia Minor revolted against Persian rule. This was known as the Ionian Revolt, and the movement was supported by Athens and Eretria. (The Editors of Encyclopaedia Britannica, 2024, sec. *The Ionian Revolt*). This prompted a swift and brutal retaliation from the Persians, launching a full-blown invasion of Greece in 490 B.C.E. This culminated in the Battle of Marathon, where Athenian forces dealt a crushing blow to the Persians.

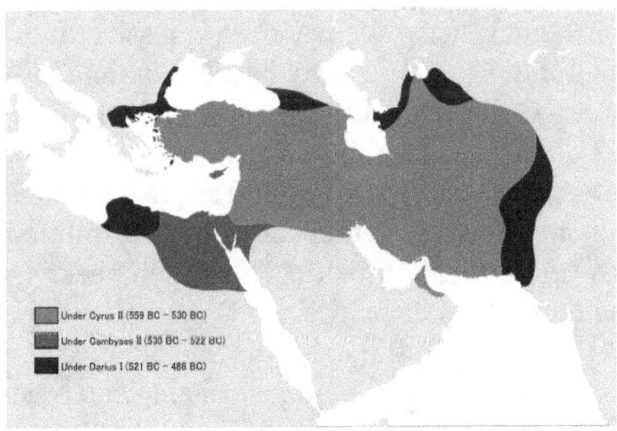

The expansion of the Persian Empire
down to the Greco-Persian Wars (Zifan, 2015).

Following the victory at Marathon, the Greek city-states realized that the Persian threat, although subdued for the time being, remained imminent. They set their differences aside in favor of a collective defense. In a rare moment of unity, the city-states, led by Athens and Sparta, created the Hellenic League and pledged to cooperate against the Persian threat.

The peak of the Persian War came about in 480 B.C.E. when the Persians launched a second invasion of Greece led by King Xerxes I (Carey, 2021). Bound by the Hellenic League, the Greek city-states rallied together to defend their homeland against overwhelming odds. The iconic battle at Thermopylae, where a small force of three hundred Spartans led a meager nine thousand allies to hold off the gargantuan Persian advance. Then, at Salamis, the Athenian navy delivered a massive blow to Persian forces. These two battles, among others, showcased the resilience and determination of the Greek alliance.

Despite these amazing victories, the alliance was fragile and held together only by the immediate threat of a Persian invasion. After the Greek victory at the Battle of Plataea in 479 B.C.E. put the threat to rest (temporarily), the cracks in the alliance started to show. Old rivalries began resurfacing and renewed conflicts and power struggles afflicted the Greek city-states.

The peace achieved at the end of the Persian Wars was short-lived, as Athens, the dominant naval power, and Sparta, the preeminent land power, found themselves locked in the bitter struggle for dominance known as the Peloponnesian Wars. The period of hot and cold conflict took place between 431 B.C.E. and 404 B.C.E. (Thucydides, 1.23–1.24). Sparta's objective was to free the states under Athenian dominion by dismantling its defenses and deconstructing its organizational framework. The extended conflict highlights the transient nature of Greek alliances and the tendency of the city-states to prioritize their interests above unity.

Athens, the birthplace of democracy, prided itself on its democratic institutions where male citizens could participate in decision-making through assemblies and elected officials. On the other hand, Sparta was renowned for its militaristic society and oligarchic government. Emphasis was placed on discipline, austerity, and military strength. The formidable power of the Spartan army made them an intimidating rival to Athens and other city-states, leading to frequent power struggles and conflicts.

The Peloponnesian Wars ended in 404 B.C.E. after the defeat of the Athenian fleet at Aegospotami (Cartwright, 2025). Sparta's terms of surrender severely weakened Athenian democracy, as Sparta rose to become the dominant power in the region. This power shift ultimately degraded many of the other city-states in the region, signaling the end of what is known as the Golden Age of Ancient Greece. In doing so, the stage was set for the rise of Macedonia.

Philip II of Macedon: The Architect of Macedonian Power

One of the most important developments in Macedonian history took place in the 7th century B.C.E. when the Argead Dynasty rose to prominence (World History Edu, 2024, sec. *What was the Argead Dynasty?*). King Perdiccas I is traditionally considered the founder of the Argeads, and under his rule Macedonia began to expand its influence beyond its early borders.

The reign of Philip II, beginning in 359 B.C.E., marked a pivotal period in Macedonian history. Born in either 383 or 382, Philip was the youngest son of King Amyntas III and Eurydice of Lynkestis. Philip's eldest brother, Alexander II, succeeded their father

Amyntas. However, after Alexander's murder, Philip was sent as a hostage to Illyria and was later held in Thebes. This is where he received a military and diplomatic education from the great Theban general and tactician Epaminondas.

Upon his return to Macedonia, Philip's other brother, King Perdiccas III, died in battle against the Illyrians. Before passing, Perdiccas appointed Philip as regent for his infant son Amyntas IV. Philip, a shrewd strategist and diplomat, succeeded in deposing his young nephew in 359 B.C.E. Known for his military innovations and political cunning, Philip was able to push the Macedonian army into the forefront of military technology within the first 10 years of his reign (Hemingway & Hemingway, 2004).

Philip II of Macedon (Mortel, 2017)

Philip II's Revolutionary Military Reforms

When Philip II ascended the throne, Macedon was a fragmented and vulnerable kingdom facing threats on multiple fronts. Recognizing that survival depended on military strength, Philip undertook a comprehensive overhaul of the Macedonian army, transforming it from a loosely organized peasant levy into a professional fighting force (Schumate, 2015).

Philip began by recruiting a dedicated core of soldiers and equipping them with standardized gear—bronze helmets, greaves, tall boots, and tunics—thereby replacing the traditional, self-equipped hoplites who had to bear the burden of heavy, cumbersome armor. This shift lightened the load on his infantry while offering uniformity in training and tactics.

A cornerstone of Philip's reforms was the introduction of the *sarissa*, a long spear between 18 and 23 feet long. This weapon supplanted the shorter *dory* of traditional hoplites, allowing Macedonian infantry to engage enemies from a safer distance. The sarissa's design—featuring an iron tip for effective penetration and a heavy counterweight for balance—necessitated a rethinking of battlefield formations. Therefore, Philip restructured the traditional phalanx into a far more disciplined and compact formation.

His reformed Macedonian Phalanx featured soldiers arranged in rows of eight across and sixteen deep—forming units of 128 men—who carried smaller forearm-strapped shields than the larger and heavier *hoplon* of older phalanxes. As the Macedonian phalanx advanced, the front-line troops held their sarissas upright until just before contact, then lowered them into an overlapping "iron wall" of spear points. This innovation created a formidable offensive thrust and a nearly impregnable barrier against enemy attacks from the front.

Yet Philip's vision extended well beyond the infantry. He reorganized the cavalry by establishing the elite Companion cavalry, or *hetairoi*—a highly trained and heavily armored unit designed for rapid, decisive shock charges that played a critical role in breaking enemy formations and exploiting gaps created by the phalanx. In addition, Philip unified the various branches of his military—infantry, cavalry, and light skirmishers—into a cohesive, flexible fighting force, enabling his troops to adapt dynamically to the challenges of the battlefield.

Finally, recognizing that innovation on the battlefield required robust support behind the lines, he instituted standardized training, strict discipline, and efficient administrative practices. His reforms in logistics and command structure ensured rapid mobilization and sustained military operations, setting new benchmarks for military organization.

Philip's reforms laid the groundwork for one of history's most formidable armies, a legacy that Alexander the Great inherited and further refined. He would become one of the most famous cavalry commanders in history with his Companions cavalry, and he perfected the robust combined arms system that integrated a disciplined phalanx with mobile cavalry and supporting troops. The Macedonian army was a professional, well-organized force whose standardization, training, and logistical efficiencies ensured Alexander was always battle-ready and capable of rapid, sustained campaigns.

For the moment, however, Philip II's military reforms revitalized Macedon and forged the foundations of a military system that would create an empire. His innovations—from the revolutionary sarissa-armed phalanx to the elite cavalry and integrated command structure—transformed Macedonian warfare and left an indelible mark on the art of war. Had they not been eclipsed by the future success of his son, Philip's innovations would surely have garnered much more popular recognition.

Diplomacy and Military Expansion

During Philip's reign, threats loomed from numerous fronts—Illyrians to the west, Thracians to the east, Paeonioans to the north, and entanglements to the south in mainland Greece. These challenges often overlapped, leading Philip to engage in multiple campaigns simultaneously. Many Greek powers were involved in the Third Sacred War, while Philip focused on the Conquest of Chalcidice along the Aegean's north coast, as well as campaigns in Thrace, alongside his participation in the Sacred War.

A notable aspect of his reign is the lack of clear documentation for many major battles. The absence of names, locations, and other important details shroud significant events in mystery, such as the battle where his brother, Perdiccas III, died, resulting in Philip's ascension to the throne. These uncertainties regarding the chronology of events in the early phase of his reign persist.

Philip assumed the throne during a crisis but swiftly addressed external threats, negotiating peace with Macedon's neighboring powers and solidifying his alliances with strategic marriages. His diplomatic and military successes are a testament to his proactive approach to governance.

The War for Amphipolis (357–356 B.C.E.) and the Social War (357–355 B.C.E.), alongside the Third Sacred War (356–346 B.C.E.), constituted a pivotal period in Greek history, marked by shifting alliances, military campaigns, and political upheaval. These conflicts were instrumental in reshaping the balance of power in Greece and ultimately led to significant diplomatic developments that had far-reaching consequences for the Greek world.

The War for Amphipolis erupted in 357 B.C.E. when Philip seized the opportunity to expand his influence by targeting Amphipolis, a strategically significant city on the border between Thessaly and Macedon (Rickard, December 2016). Amphipolis had safeguarded Philip's internal adversaries, prompting this aggressive move. Philip's Siege of Amphipolis was notable for the advanced techniques he employed, leading to the city's swift capture. Despite Athenian efforts to aid Amphipolis, their response was delayed, and the city fell before they could intervene effectively. The war triggered further hostilities between Athens and Philip, laying the groundwork for prolonged conflict in the region.

Meanwhile, the Social War unfolded in tandem, lasting from 357–355 B.C.E. This conflict came about from the internal discontent within the Athenian-led Second Athenian League, with several member states rebelling against Athenian supremacy. The war saw Athens facing revolts among its allies, particularly in the Hellespont region. The alliance with the Thracian king Cersobleptes played a crucial role in Athens' attempt to suppress the uprisings, but their efforts were thwarted by Philip's advances and shifting alliances in the region (Rickard, November 2016).

Among these regional conflicts, the Third Sacred War emerged in 356 B.C.E., which added another layer of complexity to the political landscape. This war stemmed from a dispute between Thebes and Phocis over alleged sacrilege at the Oracle of Delphi. Philip initially remained uninvolved, but he would soon be drawn in as the conflict escalated (Lau, n.d.).

The Phocian commander Onomarchus, allied with Lycophron, posed a significant threat to other Thessalian factions, prompting their appeal for Philip's assistance. Despite initial setbacks, Philip's eventual victory at the Battle of the Crocus Field in 353 or 352 B.C.E. marked a turning point in the conflict, solidifying his influence in Thessaly and securing his position as the leader of the Thessalian League.

The climax of these interconnected conflicts culminated in the Peace of Philocrates, a significant diplomatic agreement brokered in 346 B.C.E. (Rickard, January 2017). Negotiated by the Athenian statesman Philocrates, the peace treaty aimed to end the ongoing hostilities between Athens and Macedon. Under the treaty's terms, Athens recognized Macedonian power over the Greek city-states, effectively handing over its dominance in the region. Additionally, Athens agreed to join Philip in his proposed campaign against Persia, aligning their interests in the face of external threats.

The Peace of Philocrates represented a logical decision by Athens to seek reconciliation with Macedon, acknowledging the shifting power dynamics in Greece. For Philip, the treaty solidified his position as the dominant political and military force on the mainland, paving the way for his ambitious campaigns in the years to come—including his conquest of the Persian Empire.

The Stage Is Set

Alexander came of age in a world meticulously crafted by Philip II of Macedon. Against the backdrop of Macedonian power and the rich heritage of Greek culture, the stage is set for a protagonist unlike any other. On this historically fertile ground, a young prince steps into the light, poised to leave his mark.

Alexander's story begins in a world on the brink of transformation.

The next chapter will further explore the early life of Alexander – his birth, education, and friendships. Moreover, it will discuss several of the relationships that influenced him at all stages of his life, particularly his mother, Olympias, and his several wives.

Chapter 2: The Making of a King

How does a child born into ancient royalty grow to leave a lasting impact on the world? The story of Alexander the Great begins well before his legendary battles and conquests. It begins with prophecies, an influcntial mother, and a thoroughly Hellenized education.

Alexander was blessed with an extraordinary lineage. As we saw in the previous chapter, his father, Philip II, was a shrewd and ambitious ruler who had elevated Macedon from obscurity to dominance in the Greek world. His mother, Olympias, was no less formidable. Descended from the royal bloodline of Epirus and rumored to be a devotee of the mystic cult of Dionysus, Olympias instilled in her son a sense of destiny and divine purpose ("Olympias," n.d.).

Alexander's Legendary Birth

Biblical Prophecy

According to later Jewish and Christian tradition, a prophecy concerning Alexander the Great is found in the Book of Daniel 8:5–8 and 21–22. This passage is part of a vision that the prophet Daniel received, which included a symbolic representation of various kingdoms and rulers that would arise in the future. The prophet saw a vision of a male goat with a prominent horn between its eyes charging across the earth without touching the ground.

This vision is interpreted for Daniel by an angel who explains that the male goat represents the king of Greece, and the large horn between its eyes is the first king. This king would be succeeded by four notable successors, though not with the same level of power and influence as the first king. This part of the prophecy corresponded to the disintegration of Alexander's empire after his death into four successor kingdoms known as the Diadochi (Griego, 2023). Unfortunately, the dating of Daniel is controversial – tradition maintains a 6th century B.C.E. authorship, but many scholars place it in the 2nd century, well after Alexander's life. Nevertheless, for many, the tradition played an important part in forming the popular perception of Alexander in the aftermath of his conquests.

Alexander's Birth

According to ancient accounts, the night Alexander was born in 356 B.C.E., a significant event occurred at the temple of Artemis in Ephesus; it was said to have been destroyed by fire. This event was interpreted as an omen, signifying the extraordinary destiny that lay before the newborn prince (Pollard & Pollard, 2019).

In ancient cultures such as Macedon, omens and prophecies were deeply rooted in everyday life. They were believed to be messages from the gods, guiding the course of events and foretelling the fates of individuals. The destruction of the temple of Artemis at the precise moment of Alexander's birth was seen as a clear indication that he was marked by the divine, destined for greatness and world-changing deeds.

Other signs accompanied his birth. "To Philip, however, who had just taken (the city of) Potidaea, there came three messages at the same time: the first that Parmenio had conquered the Illyrians in a great battle, the second that his race-horse had won a victory at the Olympic games, while a third announced the birth of Alexander. These things delighted him, of course, and the seers raised his spirits still higher by declaring that the son whose birth coincided with three victories would be always victorious" (Plutarch, Alexander 3.4-5).

Among the Macedonian court and nobility, the prophecy inspired awe and reverence. Alexander was not just another royal heir but a figure of mythic proportions, foretold to achieve feats beyond the capabilities of ordinary mortals. His birth was celebrated as a momentous event, heralding the dawn of a new era in Macedonian history.

Even beyond the borders of Macedonia, the prophecy of Alexander's birth captured the imagination of neighboring kingdoms and distant lands. Tales of the young prince marked by the gods spread far and wide, sparking curiosity and speculation about the future that lay in store for him. Even at a young age, Alexander received Persian embassies while Philip was away on campaign. He impressed them with his incisive questions to the point that they felt he would one day surpass his father (Plutarch, Alexander 5.1).

But perhaps nowhere were the expectations for Alexander's future more pressing than within Alexander himself. He grew up aware of the prophecies surrounding his birth and the weight of expectation that it placed upon him. They instilled in him a sense of purpose and destiny, driving him to prove himself worthy of the divine favor bestowed upon him.

The Political, Cultural, and Military Backdrop

By the time the Peace of Philocrates was brokered, Alexander was a boy of 10. He grew up in Macedon against the backdrop of a politically turbulent, culturally vibrant, and militarily competitive period in Ancient Greece. He entered a world shaped by the legacies of great empires, shifting alliances, and dynamic cultural exchanges. Under the leadership of his father, Macedon emerged as a rising power, directly challenging the dominance of the southern Greek states. Through shrewd diplomacy and strategic alliances, Philip consolidated his authority, expanded Macedonian territory, and forged a unified kingdom.

At the same time, Philip II's military reforms revolutionized Macedonian warfare and transformed the Macedonian army into a highly disciplined and formidable force. His strategic alliances and diplomatic advances secured Macedon's northern and eastern borders, while his expansionist campaigns extended Macedonian influence into Thrace, Illyria, and parts of mainland Greece.

Culturally, the Greek world had enjoyed flourishing intellectual and artistic achievements throughout the 5th century. The legacy of Classical Greece, with its emphasis on philosophy, literature, and the arts, continued to influence society and shape intellectual discourse for decades. In Athens, philosophers like Plato and Aristotle laid the foundations of Western philosophy, while playwrights like Euripides and Sophocles produced timeless works of drama and tragedy.

However, in Macedon during Alexander's youth, cultural exchanges with Greek city-states enriched the northern kingdom's intellectual and artistic landscape. Under Philip's patronage, Macedonian artists and craftsmen adopted Greek artistic styles and techniques, creating a fusion of Macedonian and Hellenic artistic traditions. The royal court at Pella became a center of cultural patronage, attracting poets, artists, and scholars from across Greece and the Near East (Griffith, n.d.).

Life at Court

Life at the Macedonian court during Alexander's youth was characterized by a blend of royal protocol, military discipline, and cultural sophistication. As the son of King Philip II and Queen Olympias, Alexander grew up in an environment shaped by the traditions of Macedonian royalty and the influence of Greek culture.

At the heart of the Macedonian court was the royal palace, where Alexander and his family resided. The palace served as the hub of political activity, hosting courtiers, diplomats, and foreign dignitaries who sought an audience with the king. Within its opulent halls, Alexander was exposed to the intricacies of court etiquette. There, he witnessed the pomp and ceremony associated with royal functions.

Military training was another central aspect of life at the Macedonian court, reflecting the martial ethos of Macedonian society. From a young age, Alexander was immersed in the rigors of military education, undergoing physical training and instruction in the art of war. Under the tutelage of seasoned warriors and military commanders, he learned the principles of combat, tactics, and strategy, preparing him for his future role as a warrior king.

Bust of Alexander (Nguyen, 2017)

Despite the emphasis on martial prowess, the Macedonian court was also a center of cultural refinement and intellectual pursuits. Influenced by the ideals of Greek civilization, Philip sought to promote the arts, literature, and philosophy within his realm. As a result, Alexander was exposed to the works of Greek poets, playwrights, and philosophers, fostering a deep appreciation for the intellectual achievements of the Greek world that would stay with him through his entire life (Biography.com Editors, 2021).

Social events and festivities were also integral to life at the Macedonian court, providing opportunities for cultural exchange and diplomatic networking. Banquets, feasts, and celebrations were hosted regularly, where guests were treated to lavish entertainment, music, and culinary delights. These gatherings served not only as occasions for leisure and recreation but also as forums for political intrigue and alliance-building among the nobility. Against this backdrop of opulence and power, Alexander grew into a young prince infused with the ideals of Greek culture, the martial spirit of Macedonian tradition, and the intellectual curiosity that would define his legacy as one of history's greatest conquerors.

The Character and Ambitions of Olympias

Alexander and Olympias from a public statue in Vienna (PictureObelix, 2013)

Alexander's mother, Olympias, was born in Epirus in 375 B.C.E. Originally named Myrtale, it is believed that her name was later changed in honor of Philip's victory in the Olympic Games of 356 B.C.E. Olympias was not merely a royal consort but a formidable figure in her own right. As the daughter of King Neoptolemus I of Epirus, she inherited her father's lineage and his assertive and commanding nature. Known for her passionate and authoritative demeanor, Olympias had remarkable staying power. She even held considerable influence in the tumultuous power struggles ensuing after the deaths of Philip II and her son Alexander the Great (Wasson, 2015).

Central to Olympias's character was her deep involvement in the mystical cults of her time. Particularly notable was her affiliation with the hedonistic snake-worshiping cult of Dionysus, a deity associated with ecstasy, fertility, and divine revelation. Olympia's devotion reflected her profound belief in the potency of divine forces and her own divine descent. She eagerly passed on this belief to her son, instilling in him a sense of his own divine lineage.

The impact Olympias had on Alexander's aspirations and perspective is immeasurable. Through her guidance and teachings, Alexander was captivated by the legendary stories of figures such as Achilles, whom he regarded as a pillar of divine favor and strength. This belief in his divine heritage fueled Alexander's self-perception as a figure destined for greatness; not merely the son of Philip II, but a descendant of the gods themselves.

Olympias' ambitions were shaped by personal, familial, and political considerations aimed at securing power, influence, and prestige within the complex and competitive world of ancient Macedonian politics. She was deeply invested in securing a prominent role for Alexander in Macedonian politics and succession, and she actively promoted his interests. Olympias viewed Alexander as the primary vehicle through which her own influence could expand (Liao, 2024).

Olympias' Role in Macedonian Politics

Olympias' marriage to Philip II in 357 B.C.E. was a strategic political alliance as well as a personal union. The marriage solidified the relationship between Macedonia and Epirus, enhancing Philip's position among neighboring kingdoms and strengthening his political influence. Olympias's ties to the royal family of Epirus brought valuable connections and resources to Philip's court.

She always found managed to exert her influence on Macedonian affairs. She was known for her intelligence, charisma, and manipulative tactics, which she used to sway the opinions of courtiers and politicians alike. Olympias' ability to influence decision-making behind closed doors made her a formidable player in the political arena.

A central focus of her political maneuvering was the advancement of Alexander within the Macedonian court, often to the detriment of Philip's other wives and children (polygamy being common among Macedonian royalty). She played a crucial role in shaping Alexander's education, instilling a sense of his divine destiny in him and preparing him for future leadership. Her ambition for Alexander's success was intertwined with her own aspirations.

After the tumultuous events surrounding Philip II's assassination in 336 B.C.E., which stirred rumors implicating Olympias, the power dynamics within Macedon shifted dramatically (Carney, 1992). With Alexander ascending to the throne and embarking on his ambitious campaigns, Olympias became an even more prominent figure in Macedonian politics, assuming a *de facto* leadership role during her son's absence. Despite being physically distant from Alexander's traveling court (i.e., the center of power), Olympias maintained a strong presence in Macedon through regular correspondence with her son. Her letters to him likely contained a mix of maternal advice, political counsel, and encouragement that reinforced their bond and her influence over him.

In her pursuit of Alexander's ascension and greatness, Olympias was willing to take drastic measures, even if it meant resorting to violence or intrigue. Historical accounts suggest she may have been involved in eliminating individuals perceived as obstacles to Alexander's rise, further highlighting the lengths she was willing to go to secure her son's position (The Editors of Encyclopaedia Britannica, Olympias, 2025).

A Royal Education

Bust of Aristotle from the *Museo nazionale romano di palazzo Altemps* (Jastrow, 2006)

The influence of Greek culture on Alexander's upbringing cannot be overstated. From the epic poems of Homer to the tragedies of Aeschylus and Sophocles, Greek literature provided Alexander with a window into the human condition, inspiring him with tales of heroism, valor, and the pursuit of glory (*kleos*).

The beauty of Greek sculpture, exemplified by masterpieces like the Parthenon friezes and the sculptures of Praxiteles captivated Alexander's imagination and instilled in him an eye for aesthetic perfection. Moreover, Greek traditions informed his actions as a military leader and statesman. Inspired by the heroic deeds of Achilles and the conquests of Cyrus the Great, Alexander embarked on his own epic campaigns to conquer the known world. Some scholars believe he sought to emulate the feats of his legendary predecessors and establish a universal empire based on Greek ideals of freedom, democracy, and cultural unity (Liebert, 2011).

Aristotle's Lasting Influence

As the future king, Alexander's experience of Greek culture was not second-hand. His personal education by Aristotle is particularly significant, as it shaped his worldview, intellectual development, and approach to governance. At the Temple of the Nymphs near Naoussa, Alexander received an all-inclusive education alongside the children of Macedonian nobles, where he immersed himself in Aristotle's teachings.

Aristotle's teachings covered a spectrum of disciplines, from philosophy and ethics to science, politics, and warfare. In philosophy, he introduced Alexander to the works of Plato and prominent earlier thinkers of the Golden Age. Aristotle also instructed Alexander in rhetoric and oratory, skills that would serve him well in his future diplomatic and political endeavors. Furthermore, Aristotle provided Alexander with a solid foundation in the natural sciences, including biology, astronomy, and physics. This fostered Alexander's curiosity about the natural world and his desire for empirical understanding.

Aristotle's influence on Alexander's thinking and strategies was profound and far-reaching; Alexander developed a strategic mindset grounded in logic, reason, and careful analysis. His teacher's emphasis on moderation and balance likely contributed to Alexander's measured approach to governance and decision-making, and his teachings on ethics and virtue instilled in Alexander a sense of duty and responsibility toward his subjects, guiding his conduct as a ruler. Further, Aristotle's emphasis on rational inquiry and empirical observation laid the groundwork for Alexander's pioneering efforts in geographical exploration and scientific discovery.

This royal education gave Alexander a rigorous intellectual framework that allowed the young kind to be conversant (perhaps even excellent) in nearly every field he would need as king. Moreover, this broad-based education cultivated Alexander's intellectual curiosity and fostered a deep appreciation for Greek culture and its intellectual heritage.

Indeed, Aristotle's influence endured beyond Alexander's lifetime. Through the young king, it shaped the intellectual and cultural landscape of the

Hellenistic world that emerged in the wake of Alexander's conquests, and Aristotle's ideas continued to resonate with scholars and thinkers for centuries, leaving a lasting legacy extending far beyond the confines of ancient Macedonia (Wu, 2022).

Alexander's Family and Friends

Philip II

The relationship between Alexander and his father was complex and multifaceted, characterized by deep admiration and strained tensions. Initially, Alexander held his father Philip in high regard and sought to emulate him. Growing up in the royal court of Macedonia, Alexander was exposed to Philip's military prowess, political acumen, and ambition for expanding Macedonian power.

Alexander accompanied his father at the Battle of Chaeronea in 338 when he was only 18. His father put him in command of the cavalry on the left wing, which he led with distinction. This victory ended Greek resistance on the mainland and resulted in Philip's becoming *hegemon* of the Hellenic League in preparation for invading Persia (The Editors of Encyclopaedia Britannica, n.d.). These experiences gave Alexander a deep respect for his father and a desire to prove himself worthy of Philip's legacy.

As Alexander matured and his ambitions began to emerge, tension developed between father and son. Philip's multiple marriages and dalliances with other women, including his relationship with Cleopatra Eurydice, caused friction within the royal family. In particular, they strained the King's relationship with Alexander's mother, Olympias. Evidence suggests that Philip recognized Alexander's potential and respected his abilities as a leader. However, this could have been both a source of bride and jealousy – did Philip want to groom Alexander as his successor, or remove a potential rival?

Tragically, any resolution to the complexities of their relationship was cut short by Philip's assassination in 336 B.C.E., when Alexander was only 20 years old. Alexander and Olympias were not above suspicion (Carney, 1992). Nevertheless, the sudden loss of his father thrust Alexander into the spotlight as the new king of Macedonia. He was forced to navigate the challenges of succession and consolidate his power in the wake of his father's death.

Thessalonike

Thessalonike was the daughter of Philip and his Thessalian wife, Nicesipolis. She was Alexander's half-sister, sharing a common father but having different mothers. Her name was given to her in honor of Philip's defeat of the Thessalians.

While there is limited information available about their relationship, they likely shared at least some level of familiarity and interaction due to their shared royal status. She was no older than seven when Alexander left for his campaign against the Persians, but it appears that the young princess was raised by her stepmother Olympias.

After Alexander's death in 323 B.C.E., a struggle for dominion over his empire broke out. Thessalonike was married to Cassander, one of Alexander's generals, who became a prominent figure. As Alexander the Great's sister, her marriage to Cassander helped legitimize his rule. Thessalonike learned well from Olympias and raised her own royal children: Philip IV of Macedon, Antipater I of Macedon, and Alexander V of Macedon. Like her stepmother, she attempted to manipulate her children to her own advantage, essentially so that she could rule with them after Cassander's death (Choubineh, 2024).

Alexander's Early Companions

In Alexander's formative years, a group of young companions emerged who would not only accompany him throughout his legendary campaigns but also become key figures in shaping his destiny. Among them were Perdiccas, Leonnatus, Ptolemy, Hephaistion, and Cassander. Their bonds, forged in the crucible of their youth, proved instrumental in the conquests and challenges that lay ahead of them.

Alexander's relationship with Perdiccas, a noble Macedonian general, was marked by mutual trust, respect, and camaraderie. From their earliest campaigns together, Perdiccas proved himself to be a steadfast and capable commander, earning Alexander's admiration and confidence. As one of Alexander's most trusted advisors, Perdiccas held positions of high authority within the Macedonian army, serving as a key confidant to the young king. After Alexander's death, Perdiccas played a crucial role in the governance of Macedonia, validating Alexander's assessment of his long-time friend.

Another noble Macedonian general, Leonnatus distinguished himself early on as a skilled and courageous warrior, earning Alexander's respect. Throughout their campaigns together, Leonnatus proved himself to be an invaluable asset, demonstrating martial prowess and unwavering dedication to his king. Their bond was forged on the battlefield, with Leonnatus standing by Alexander's side in the heat of battle and serving as a trusted advisor and confidant.

Alexander's relationship with Ptolemy began in their youth. They shared a friendship forged in the halls of education and the fields of training. Both hailing from noble Macedonian families, they were brought together under the tutelage of Aristotle, where they received an education befitting their royal status. Ptolemy's keen intellect and leadership abilities quickly caught Alexander's attention, and a bond of mutual respect and friendship began to blossom. As they grew older, their relationship deepened, strengthened by their shared experiences on the battlefield and in the corridors of power.

Ptolemy's unwavering loyalty and sound judgment made him a valued advisor to Alexander, and their friendship would endure to the end of Alexander's life.

The relationship between Alexander and Hephaistion was a profound and enduring bond that began in their youth and continued until Hephaistion's untimely death. From their early years in Macedon, Hephaistion was Alexander's closest friend and companion. He also shared in an education under Aristotle and Alexander's military campaigns across Asia.

Hephaistion was Alexander's confidant and his most trusted advisor and ally. Their relationship transcended mere friendship and was characterized by a deep emotional connection and mutual respect. Despite Hephaistion's humble origins compared to Alexander's royal lineage, their bond remained unshakeable, and Hephaistion held a position of unparalleled influence within Alexander's inner circle. His death devastated Alexander, who mourned him deeply and honored his memory with extravagant funeral rites. The relationship between Alexander and Hephaistion is one of the most enduring and celebrated friendships in history, symbolizing loyalty, devotion, and companionship (Hays, 2024).

A Legacy in the Making

In this chapter, we explored the early life and formative influences that shaped Alexander the Great's remarkable journey from prince to conqueror. We discussed into the prophecies surrounding his birth and the formidable influence of his mother, Olympias, whose passionate nature and involvement in mystical cults left an indelible mark on Alexander's ambitions and worldview. We examined the pivotal role of Aristotle as Alexander's tutor, whose teachings in philosophy, ethics, and strategy laid the foundation for his intellectual development and strategic prowess.

We also explored Alexander's relationships with key figures in his life, including his close companions, who would prove instrumental in his conquests and the challenges that lay ahead. Among them, the bond between Alexander and Hephaistion stands out as a profound and enduring friendship, characterized by mutual respect, loyalty, and emotional connection.

Alexander's marriages to Roxane, Stateira, and Parysatis served both political and symbolic purposes in consolidating his rule over his vast empire as well as bridging the gap between Macedonians and Persians. These marriages reflect Alexander's strategic pragmatism, his ambition for imperial unity, and his openness to cultural exchange.

With prophecy, maternal ambition, and an exceptional education laying the groundwork, Alexander stood on the brink of greatness. However, it was the abrupt and profound change in Macedon's political landscape that propelled him into prominence. As we move from Alexander's upbringing to his rise to power, we explore the pivotal events that mark the start of his journey to become history's most renowned conqueror.

Chapter 3: Accession to the Throne

Alexander's ascent to the throne was not just a transition of power, it was the beginning of a new era. As dawn broke over the ancient city of Pella, the capital of Macedon, whispers of uncertainty filled the air. With the demise of King Philip II, the once-stable kingdom teetered on the brink of chaos, its fate hanging in the balance. This chapter explores the accession of Alexander to the Macedonian throne, highlighting the qualities that will mark his career as conqueror and emperor.

The King is Dead, Long Live the King

Philip's Assassination

In 336 B.C.E., Philip was at the height of his power. Only two years prior he had won the battle of Chaeronea, making him the master of Greece due to his diplomatic and military superiority. Philip's next goal was to lead a united Greek front against the Persians; however, it never came to pass.

A wedding feast was held in Aegae, in Macedon, to celebrate the marriage of Philip's daughter Cleopatra. Philip arranged her marriage to Alexander I of Epirus to cement diplomatic relations between the two kingdoms (*Alexander the Great's Sister: Cleopatra of Macedonia (354-308 BC)*, 2022). Nobles, generals, and dignitaries from across the realm gathered to celebrate the union, along with prominent players in Philip's court.

Despite ongoing domestic turmoil in the royal household, Olympias was also in attendance. The relationship between Philip and Olympias was strained due to accusations of adultery and Philp's allegations that Alexander was not his legitimate son. Years later, it was even rumored that Olympias had orchestrated the assassination of Cleopatra Eurydice, Philip's new bride, along with her infant daughter, in order to secure Alexander's claim to the throne. To be sure, Olympias' presence at the festivities added an undercurrent of tension (The Editors of Encyclopaedia Britannica, 2025, January 1).

During the banquet, Pausanias, one of Philip's bodyguards, approached the king and plunged his sword deep into the king's chest, fatally wounding him. As chaos erupted, Pausanias fled the banquet despite efforts to apprehend him by guests and Philip's other bodyguards. Pausanias sought refuge with Attalus, a longtime friend of Philip's and fellow bodyguard. Attalus wished to distance himself from the assassination and refused to take Pausanias in.

Feeling abandoned and desperate, Pausanias fled to a nearby shrine for sanctuary. However, he was eventually captured and killed by Philip's loyal supporters, who sought justice for their slain king. Pausanias's motives for assassinating Philip remain a subject of speculation, with some theories suggesting personal grievances or political motivations.

One theory is that Olympias orchestrated Philip's assassination. Conflicts, infidelities, and power struggles marked their marriage. Olympias may have harbored resentment towards Philip for his mistreatment of her and his perceived favoritism towards other wives and concubines. Along with the rumors of Olympias' involvement in the deaths of Cleopatra Eurydice and her daughter, it's believed that she may also have ordered the assassination of Philip to secure Alexander's position and fast-track his rise to power, thereby securing her own position in the Macedonian court (Carney, 1992).

Given the volatile nature of Macedonian politics at the time, the theory that Philip's assassination was politically motivated is widely accepted among historians. Within the Macedonian court, there were rival factions vying for influence and power. Philip's military campaigns and expansionist policies had made him both admired and feared by many of his nobles. Some members of the aristocracy may have seen his death as an opportunity to advance their own agendas or to prevent further consolidation of power under Philip's rule.

Additionally, Philip's aggressive expansionism had earned him many enemies beyond the borders of Macedon. Greek city-states, such as Athens and Thebes, viewed him as a threat to their autonomy and actively opposed his efforts to unite Greece under the Macedonian domain. It's possible that individuals or groups from these regions conspired to eliminate Philip in the hopes of destabilizing Macedon and weakening its influence in the region.

The Aftermath

News of Philip's assassination sent shockwaves throughout the Greek world, leading to significant political instability both within Macedon and among its neighboring states. Macedon suddenly found itself in a power vacuum and questions about the succession were raised. Despite his military prowess and strategic brilliance, Alexander's age and lack of experience as a ruler raised concerns about his ability to maintain control over the growing Macedonian domains.

Philip's half-brother Arrhidaeus, also known as Philip III, was another potential claimant to the throne. However, his mental and physical disabilities made him an unlikely candidate to rule independently. His claim to the throne was largely supported by those seeking to manipulate him for their own ends (*Philip Arrhidaeus*, 2020).

Silver tetradrachm depicting Philip III Arrhidaeus (CNG Coins, 2017)

Amyntas IV, the son of Philip's brother Perdiccas III, was another contender. His claim was weakened by his young age and lack of support among the Macedonian nobility. Nevertheless, he remained a potential pawn in the power struggles following Philip's assassination (*Amyntas IV of Macedon,* n.d.).

The potential for civil war loomed large in the aftermath of Philip's assassination. The power struggle threatened to plunge Macedon into chaos and weaken its ability to defend against external threats. Athens and Thebes, in particular, saw the power vacuum as a chance to challenge Macedonian supremacy and assert their influence.

Securing a Succession

Upon the assassination of his father, Alexander swiftly moved to press his claim to the throne. Despite the turmoil caused by Philip's death, Alexander's decisive actions and clear declaration of his right to rule garnered widespread support from the Macedonian nobility and army. His proclamation as king was met without opposition, showing the respect and recognition of his authority (Goldsworthy, 2023).

In addition, Alexander demonstrated political acumen and diplomatic skill in navigating the complex power dynamics of the Macedonian court. His first priority was to nurture close ties with the influential nobles and military generals who wielded influence within Macedon. Through personal charm, charisma, and a keen understanding of each individual's ambitions and interests, Alexander forged strong bonds with these key figures. He demonstrated respect for their status and incorporated their advice into his decision-making.

Alexander also recognized the importance of extending his network of connections beyond the confines of the Macedonian court. He actively sought out alliances with regional leaders, neighboring kingdoms, and foreign powers, recognizing that a strong external network could bolster his legitimacy and provide additional sources of support in times of need. This allowed him to neutralize potential sources of opposition and strengthened his position as the legitimate successor to his father's throne.

Additionally, Alexander embarked on a series of military campaigns to suppress any rebellions or dissenting factions within Macedon. He swiftly crushed any challenges to his rule, demonstrating his willingness and ability to use military force to maintain order and stability within the kingdom.

Alexander's Vision for a New Empire

Elimination of Rivals

Upon taking the throne, Alexander wasted no time consolidating his power and eliminating any threats to his reign. He understood that the swift removal of rival claimants was essential to asserting his authority and preventing opposition within Macedon. One of the most significant actions he took in this regard was the execution of his cousin, Amyntas IV, who posed a direct challenge to his budding kingship.

The decisive action of executing Amyntas sent a clear message to any other challengers or dissenters within Macedon: Alexander was not to be contested. Opposition to his rule would be met with swift and severe consequences. This deterrence helped maintain order and stability within the kingdom as potential rivals and adversaries were discouraged from challenging Alexander's authority.

Military Campaigns and Diplomacy

Alexander's military campaigns were pivotal in expanding his empire, solidifying his grip on power, and securing his position as king of Macedon. Recognizing the importance of military might in maintaining authority, Alexander strategically employed a combination of military campaigns and diplomacy to consolidate his rule.

Alexander embarked on campaigns aimed at suppressing revolts and rebellions within Macedon and its territories. Among these was his decisive campaign against a Thracian uprising, where he quelled dissent and restored order to the region. By swiftly and decisively putting down internal opposition, Alexander demonstrated his strength and determination to maintain control over his kingdom.

Alexander also recognized the importance of asserting Macedonian dominance over the Greek city-states, which had historically been a source of contention and instability. He launched military campaigns to subdue resistance and establish Macedonian supremacy, consolidating his power over Greece. His famous campaign against Thebes was particularly significant in this regard. The swift and decisive victory at Thebes served to assert Macedonian authority and deter other Greek city-states from challenging Alexander's rule (Holmes, 2024).

Photo of the Cadmeia, the ruined fortress of Thebes (Nefasdicere, 2006)

Integration of Forces

Alexander's decision to integrate soldiers from various Greek city-states into his army marked a strategic departure from traditional Macedonian military practices. It played a crucial role in the success of his campaigns, particularly his invasion of Persia. He recognized the benefits of a diverse and integrated force, and he assembled a multinational army composed of soldiers from different Greek regions, including the Thessalian League, the League of Corinth, and mercenaries from various backgrounds (Wasson, 2023).

By incorporating soldiers from outside of Macedon, Alexander augmented his military strength with additional manpower above and beyond what Macedon could supply. Moreover, he fostered a sense of unity and loyalty among the Greek city-states. This integration served to diminish potential dissent and rebellion from these regions, as they became active participants in Alexander's vision of conquest and expansion.

One of the key advantages of integrating soldiers from other Greek city-states was the diversity of skills, tactics, and resources they brought to the table. Soldiers from different regions had specialized combat experiences, training, and knowledge of the terrain, which complemented the strengths of the Macedonian forces. This diversity enhanced the overall effectiveness and adaptability of Alexander's army, allowing it to overcome a wide range of challenges encountered during his military campaigns in Asia. With the integration of non-Macedonian forces, Alexander portrayed himself as a champion of Greek unity and liberation, rallying support from across the Hellenic world for his cause.

Later, Alexander faced chronic manpower shortages, particularly during his campaigns in Persia. He addressed this issue by incorporating Persian soldiers trained in the Macedonian style into Macedonian ranks. Integrating Persian soldiers alongside Macedonian and Greek troops bolstered Alexander's military strength and sent a powerful message to those who considered welcoming his rule (Wasson, 2023).

As a result of this approach (and his own initiative), Alexander's military campaigns were marked by their speed, daring, and strategic brilliance. His army gave him the ability to adapt to different terrains, climates, and military tactics. This, he became the master of combining cavalry, infantry, artillery, and siege engines to overcome his adversaries. He would go on to lead his armies on conquests that swept through Asia Minor, Egypt, Mesopotamia, and beyond, defeating formidable enemies such as the Persian Empire and its mighty king, Darius III. His conquests extended as far east as the borders of India, establishing one of the largest empires in history (Little, 2024).

Administrative Policies

Alexander's approach to administration in the territories he conquered was characterized by a practicality similar to how he maintained his fighting force. His tendency to adapt existing administrative structures rather than imposing entirely new systems facilitated the assimilation and management of diverse populations in Greece (Kholod, 2024). Alexander would continue this approach throughout his entire reign.

One key strategy employed by Alexander was the use of marriage to forge alliances and intermingle the conquered with the conquerors. Through strategic marriages, Alexander aimed to create bonds of loyalty and kinship between the ruling elites of conquered territories and the Macedonian nobility. This allowed him to bring local rulers and aristocrats into his inner circle, securing their allegiance and gaining valuable insights into local customs, traditions, and governing practices (*Susa Weddings*, n.d.)..

Later, Alexander would even adopt elements of Persian court culture, blending them with Macedonian traditions to create a hybrid administrative framework that reflected the diversity of his empire. This inclusive approach allowed Alexander to accommodate the cultural and administrative preferences of different regions while maintaining a degree of continuity and stability in governance.

These policies of integration and cultural hybridization were not universally embraced within Macedonian society. Many Macedonians harbored deep-seated resentment towards foreigners and viewed the merging of Greek and foreign cultures as disrespectful or threatening to their own identity. Some segments of Macedonian society resisted Alexander's attempts at unification, fearing the erosion of traditional Macedonian values and customs.

Nevertheless, by creating a unified ruling class comprising both Macedonians and local elites, Alexander aimed to foster a sense of common identity and purpose among his subjects. This unified ruling class played a crucial role in managing dissent and integrating diverse populations within the empire. This empowering local elites to participate in governance and decision-making processes helped Alexander mitigate the risk of rebellion and resistance while also promoting stability and cohesion within his empire.

The Dawn of Conquest

With the throne secured and his authority unchallenged, Alexander turned his gaze beyond the borders of Macedon, propelled by the tumultuous events that had shaped his ascent to power. Through skillful maneuvering and strategic alliances, Alexander consolidated his power, quelling dissent and forging a unified front within Macedon. Yet, his vision extended far beyond the confines of his kingdom, encompassing the vast expanse of the Persian Empire and beyond.

As Alexander prepared to confront the challenges that lay ahead, he grappled with the complexities of cultural integration and the delicate balance of power. But his ambition burned bright, igniting the flames of conquest that would soon engulf the ancient world. Amid the dust and chaos of conflict, Alexander's vision for a new empire began to assert itself.

Chapter 4: The Road to Empire

In 334 B.C.E., Alexander had compelled most of the Greeks to recognize his hegemony as they had recognized his father's. He stood at the edge of the Greek world with his 20,000 soldiers and looked east. Through a series of daring battles, he would take it upon himself to realize Philip's dream of an invasion of Persia – but it would carry him farther than he could have anticipated. The journey from the Granicus River to the city of Tyre to the sands of Gaugamela and beyond was not just a path to conquest. It was a testament to the vision, strategy, and sheer will of the young king.

The chapter ahead examines a pivotal phase of Alexander's conquest, marked by a string of remarkable victories that would cement his legacy as one of history's greatest military tacticians. As Alexander confronted some of his most formidable adversaries, every encounter left an enduring imprint on the history of warfare.

The Battle of the Granicus

The Battle of the Granicus stands as a pivotal moment, marking the beginning of Alexander's campaign against the vast Persian Empire. It was here, on the banks of the Granicus River in May 334 B.C.E., that Alexander faced his first major test of arms against the formidable forces of Darius III's

Persian governors (satraps). With the fate of his ambitions hanging in the balance, his strategic brilliance and unwavering courage were put to the test in a clash that opened the gates of the east to Macedonian forces.

The Strategic Importance of the Granicus River

The Granicus River, situated in northern present-day Turkey, held immense strategic importance for Alexander's conquest of the Persian Empire. Crossing the river was a matter of geographical necessity and a critical step in establishing Macedonian control over the western Persian territories.

Firstly, the Granicus River acted as a natural barrier, serving as an imposing obstacle that Alexander needed to overcome to advance deeper into Persian-held lands. The river's swift currents, influenced by the rugged terrain through which it flowed, made navigation challenging for anyone attempting to cross. The river's flow was often unpredictable, intensified by seasonal variations in water levels, which could transform a seemingly placid watercourse into a raging torrent during periods of heavy rainfall or snowmelt.

Additionally, the Granicus carved its path through rocky terrain, creating submerged obstacles and shifting sandbars beneath its surface. These underwater hazards posed significant risks to those attempting to cross the river, as they could easily snag boats or disrupt the passage of troops, leading to potential casualties or logistical setbacks.

The Granicus was also flanked by steep, precipitous banks, further complicating attempts to cross. The terrain surrounding the river provided ample opportunities for ambushes and defensive positions, and they allowed defenders to exploit the natural features to their advantage and repel would-be invaders.

Psychologically, the Granicus River was a symbolic gateway to Asia Minor, a region rich in resources and strategic importance. With a victory here, Alexander could gain control over key territories and encourage the many Greek city-states in Asia Minor to rebel against Persian rule, further weakening Persian influence in the region (Wasson, 2011).

Persian Forces Against Alexander

The Persian forces that Alexander faced at the Battle of the Granicus were formidable. Led by Persian satraps and accompanied by Greek mercenaries loyal to King Darius III, the Persian army comprised a diverse array of troops drawn from various regions of the Great King's empire. This multinational force brought together skilled cavalry, infantry, and chariots. It presented a multifaceted threat to Alexander's army (Wasson, 2011).

At the forefront of the Persian ranks were the Persian cavalry, renowned for their expertise in mounted warfare and their fearsome reputation on the battlefield. Led by skilled commanders, these cavalry units formed the backbone of the Persian army's offensive, capable of launching devastating charges and outmaneuvering their adversaries with speed and precision.

The Persian infantry, though perhaps not as renowned as their mounted counterparts, were nevertheless a force to be reckoned with. Drawn from many ethnic backgrounds within the empire, they brought unique strengths to the battlefield, from the disciplined ranks of the Greek mercenaries to the fierce warriors of the Persian heartlands. Infantrymen were often armed with a wide variety of weapons, ranging from spears and swords to bows and arrows. While they lacked the disciplined phalanx formations characteristic of Greek hoplites, the Persian infantry compensated with their numerical superiority and their familiarity with the local terrain. The ancient sources disagree (as on many other points of the battle and Alexander in general) on the number of men arrayed against Alexander. Estimates go from about 15,000 to 40,000, though the lower end of the range seems more likely.

The Battle

Arrian offers the most coherent description of the battle (Arrian 1.13-16). Both sides lined up on either side of the river – Persians with the cavalry at the bank and infantry behind; Alexander with his phalanx in the center and mixed cavalry and light infantry on the wings. Alexander ordered a squadron of Companions on his right to cross and attack the Persian cavalry directly across. The Persian horsemen defended the steep bank with javelins and repelled the attack. But their formation lost cohesion in the pursuit. Alexander struck.

He ordered the entire force across the river and personally led the Companions across and into the disorganized Persian cavalry, defying the counsel of his generals, who urged him to proceed with caution. Riding his famous horse, Bucephalus, Alexander spearheaded the assault. As at Chaeronea under Philip's command, his personal valor bolstered the men.

Amidst the chaos of the battlefield, Alexander found his life in grave danger. In a moment of fierce combat, he was confronted by the Persian nobleman Rhosaces, who struck Alexander on the helmet with his sword, possibly injuring him. In a display of reflexes and courage, Alexander dispatched the Persian with his lance. Soon after, Spithridates, the Persian *satrap* of Ionia and Lydia, tried to attack Alexander from behind. The young king was only saved by the timely intervention of his friend, Cleitus the Black, who hacked off the assailant's arm (Plutarch, n.d.).

Spithridates attacking Alexander from behind (Le Brun, 2019)
Cleitus intervenes from the left.

Despite the danger, Alexander continued to lead from the front, and the rest of the Macedonian force had crossed the river to gain a foothold and catch up with him. The Macedonian cavalry eventually drove off their Persian counterparts. The Companions, in particular, had an advantage in the *xyston,* a lance between 10 and 15 feet long. With it, they could strike more effectively in melee combat than the Persians with only their javelins and swords.

Without cavalry protection, the Greek mercenaries at the core of the Persian infantry faced a frontal assault by Alexander's phalanx. They resisted, but soon fell surrounded by the combined arms of the Macedonian phalangites and mixed cavalry support.

Alexander's unwavering determination and tactical prowess proved decisive, as the Macedonians secured a hard-fought victory over their adversaries. The Battle of the Granicus opened the gateway to Asia Minor for Alexander's advancing army, solidifying his foothold in the region and setting the stage for further conquests.

The Battle of Issus and Siege of Tyre

The Siege of Tyre and the Battle of Issus showcase Alexander's unparalleled military expertise and strategic genius. These two campaigns unfolded in the rugged landscapes of the ancient Near East, testing Alexander's leadership and resolve against his adversaries. From the unyielding siege of the Phoenician city of Tyre to the clash at Issus against the Persians, these events exemplify the fearlessness and determination that characterized Alexander's quest for dominion over the known world.

The Battle of Issus

The Battle of Issus, fought in 333 B.C.E., is one of the most decisive engagements in Alexander the Great's conquest of the Persian Empire. Positioned on the banks of the Pinarus River in present-day southern Turkey, the battle pitted Alexander's outnumbered Macedonian army against the forces of King Darius III, who commanded his army in person.

As recounted by Arrian, Darius III deployed a vast host, sending 30,000 cavalry and 20,000 light infantry across the Pinarus River while dispatching an additional 20,000 troops to flank Alexander's rear (Kikoy, 2018). This overwhelming numerical superiority initially posed a massive challenge for the Macedonian king.

Alexander's strategic brilliance and tactical acumen quickly turned the tide of battle. Recognizing the importance of maneuverability and exploiting the terrain to his advantage, Alexander skillfully deployed his troops. He positioned the elite Hetairoi alongside the cavalry of Thessalians and Macedonians under his command on the right flank, while the Peloponnesians, led by Philip's old general Parmenio, held the left.

The Macedonian army's disciplined phalanx formation, coupled with their aggressive cavalry charges, was again devastating against the Persian forces. Despite being outnumbered, Alexander's troops executed a series of coordinated attacks that shattered the enemy lines and caused chaos among the Persian ranks.

In the heat of battle, Alexander demonstrated unparalleled courage and leadership, leading his troops from the front and inspiring them with his boldness. His involvement in the fighting bolstered the morale of his soldiers and instilled in them a determination to achieve victory at all costs.

The decisive moment of the battle came when the Macedonian cavalry, led by Alexander and his Companions, launched an assault on the Persian center, where Darius III was stationed. In a desperate attempt to break through the Macedonian lines, Darius ordered his elite troops into the fray. However, the Macedonian phalanx held firm, and Alexander's cavalry succeeded in routing the Persian forces (Hammond, 1992).

Detail from the famous Alexander Mosaic. Originally found in the House of the Faun, Pompeii, now in *Museo Archeologico Nazionale di Napoli*. The detail depicts Alexander charging the Persian lines, directly at Darius III (Brandmeister~commonswiki, 2014).

The victory at Issus was a resounding triumph for Alexander and a testament to his military genius. Despite being outnumbered and facing a formidable adversary, Alexander's tactical acumen, along with the courage and discipline of his troops, secured a decisive victory that further solidified his dominance in the region.

The victory at Issus provided a significant morale boost to Alexander's army. It instilled in them a belief in their invincibility and set the stage for further conquests across the Persian Empire. The defeat dealt a severe blow to the prestige of Darius III and the Persian Empire, demonstrating the vulnerability of their seemingly invincible forces in the face of Alexander's persistent advance. For now, the Great King retreated to the Persian heartland to rebuild his army. Alexander wisely used the time to gain control over the western part of the Persian Empire.

The Strategic Importance of Tyre

The citadel of Tyre was nestled on a small island off the Mediterranean coast in modern day Lebanon. It held strategic significance in the ancient Near East. Serving as a crucial stronghold for the Persian fleet, the well-defended city provided a haven and a vital base for naval operations in the eastern Mediterranean. Its capture was essential for Alexander before advancing on Egypt, as leaving Tyre unconquered would expose his rear to potential threats and jeopardize the entirety of his campaign (*The Siege of Tyre (332 BCE)*, 2002).

The Siege

In 332 B.C.E., Alexander attempted to negotiate with the Tyrian leadership, seeking their surrender without bloodshed. However, the Tyrians, confident in the strength of their fortifications, defiantly rejected Alexander's proposals. Alexander swiftly initiated a blockade, cutting off Tyre from crucial supply lines and isolating the city from external support.

Alexander ordered the construction of a raised causeway to connect the mainland to the island city. Despite facing fierce resistance from the Tyrians, who launched relentless counterattacks and employed ingenious defensive tactics, Alexander's army persevered, gradually inching closer to their objective.

The prolonged siege took its toll on both the besiegers and the besieged. The Tyrians endured immense hardships as supplies dwindled and morale waned, while Alexander's army faced constant danger and fatigue from the relentless assaults. Nevertheless, Alexander's determination remained unshaken, and his troops pressed on with unwavering resolve.

After seven months, Alexander's army finally breached the walls of Tyre, overwhelming the exhausted defenders and securing victory. The fall of

Tyre was a significant triumph for Alexander, marking the culmination of months of effort and strategic maneuvering. By capturing this stronghold, Alexander managed to eliminate a formidable obstacle to his ambitions and gain control over vital maritime routes in the eastern Mediterranean. The causeway remains intact to this day.

The Battle of Gaugamela

Few battles rival the scale and significance of the Battle of Gaugamela in 331 B.C.E. on the plains of Mesopotamia. This clash between Alexander's army and the Persian Empire, led (again) by Darius III in person, stands as a defining moment in history. As the two kings collided in a dramatic showdown, the fate of the known world hung in the balance.

The Buildup to the Battle

Alexander's pursuit of the Persian Empire was fueled by an array of motivations, blending personal ambition, strategic objectives, and a historical desire for vengeance. Since ascending to the throne, Alexander had been determined to conquer the Persian Empire, recognizing the vast resources it held as essential for sustaining his ever-growing military forces and alleviating the financial burdens inherited from his predecessors. Alexander's campaign against Persia carried with it a deeply ingrained sense of historical destiny, driven by the memory of past Persian invasions of Greece, including the infamous campaigns of Darius the Great and Xerxes a century earlier.

As Alexander's forces advanced eastward, his brilliance and determination became evident. Securing the Mediterranean coasts and the conquest of Egypt were critical milestones in his march towards Persia, laying the groundwork for the confrontation to come. Throughout his journey, Alexander demonstrated a blend of military prowess and diplomatic finesse, forging alliances with local rulers and winning the loyalty of his troops through acts of courage and charisma. His progress through Syria, marked by elaborate sacrificial rituals and grand festivities, served not only to boost morale but also to signal his confidence and readiness for the impending clash with Darius III's forces.

Meanwhile, on the other side of the battlefield, Darius III was not idle. Aware of Alexander's movements and recognizing the threat posed by the Macedonian king, Darius meticulously prepared for the inevitable showdown. Selecting the plain of Gaugamela as the site of the decisive battle, Darius leveraged his knowledge of the terrain to his advantage. The plain's expansive and relatively flat layout provided an ideal battleground for the Persian cavalry and chariots, enabling them to maneuver freely and maximize their effectiveness in combat. Darius also ordered further leveling of the ground and made strategic alterations to the landscape, removing obstacles to further optimize the battlefield for his chariot forces (The Editors of Encyclopaedia Britannica, n.d.).

As Alexander and Darius converged on the plains of Gaugamela, both leaders were acutely aware of the stakes involved and the strategic imperatives driving their respective armies towards the ultimate confrontation.

The Numerical Superiority of the Persian Army

The numerical superiority of the Persian army under the command of Darius III loomed over Alexander's forces as they prepared for the clash at Gaugamela. It is widely acknowledged that the Persians held a significant numerical advantage, particularly in their cavalry forces (De Santis, 2001).

The Persian army also possessed a wide array of weaponry and military technology. Among its most fearsome assets were the scythed war chariots, designed to tear through enemy ranks and sow chaos among their adversaries. This inclusion in the Persian arsenal reflected Darius III's intent to exploit his numerical advantage and overwhelm Alexander's forces with the sheer force of numbers and innovative weaponry. His best hope of victory: surround Alexander with his overwhelming cavalry force.

Despite facing these odds, Alexander's army was characterized by its exceptional discipline, training, and leadership. Led by the visionary and tactically astute commander himself, Alexander's forces comprised a diverse array of units, each trained and equipped to counter the strengths of the Persian army.

The renowned Companion cavalry, elite infantry phalanx, and skilled light infantry and archers formed the backbone of Alexander's fighting force. These units, each playing a crucial role in the Macedonian army's overall strategy, were expertly deployed to neutralize the Persian chariots and cavalry, ensuring that Alexander's forces could effectively confront their numerically superior adversaries on the battlefield. Alexander himself commended the right half of the Macedonian line, including part of the phalanx; Parmenio the left.

The Battle

Alexander ordered the entire phalanx to advance against the Persian center. The wings of cavalry and light infantry on either side remained echeloned back slightly to receive the Persian cavalry's flanking maneuver. For his part, Darius determined to hold the Macedonian phalanx with his own center while largest cavalry force outflanked Parmenion on the Macedonian left.

Alexander recognized that Darius' best option was to surround him. Therefore, he decided to artificially lengthen his own right wing to make it appear like he was trying to outflank the Persian left. He ordered a combined force of light infantry and cavalry to launch the feint, which he commanded in person. He intended to lure the Persian cavalry into

The opening movements of Gaugamela
(The Department of History, United States Military Academy, 2006).

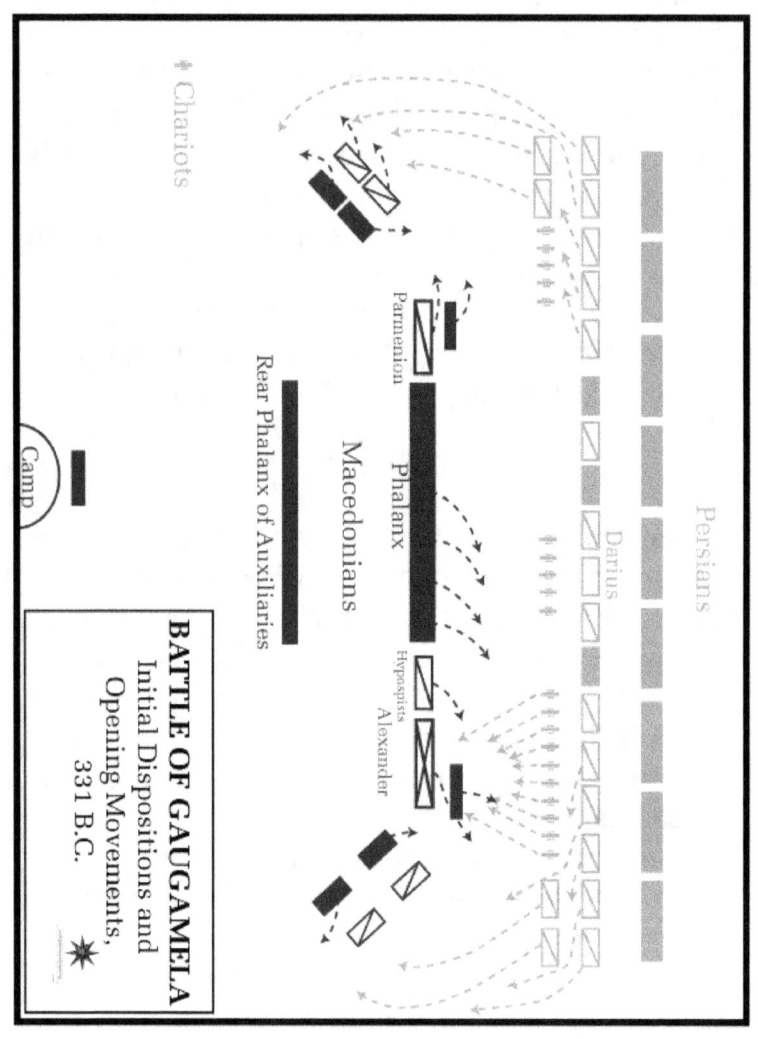

a reckless pursuit and encourage them to overextend themselves. However, the sheer number of Persians made an elongated (and thinned) Macedonian line extremely risky.

A general cavalry and light infantry engagement developed on the Macedonian right, wherein Alexander slowly introduced reserve forces bit by bit between aggressive charges with his Companions. With time and discipline, Alexander managed to stretch the Persian left all the way to the edge of the battlefield where hilly terrain made cavalry less effective. There, Alexander's light infantry became more effective. Even Darius' scythed chariots proved ineffective against the mobile javelineers of the Macedonian light infantry and elite *hypaspists* (see belof Chapter 7).

With the Persian cavalry committed to a much larger outflanking maneuver than they had initially planned, Alexander executed a massive assault where the connection between the Persian left and center was weakest. He formed every company he could find at hand into a wedge and led a furious charge with his Companions at the head. The Macedonian cavalry thundered through weakened enemy lines. The ferocity and momentum of the charge shattered the Persian center, causing chaos and confusion among their ranks.

Alexander's charge through the gap in the Persian line
(Martini & The Department of History,
United States Military Academy, 2005).

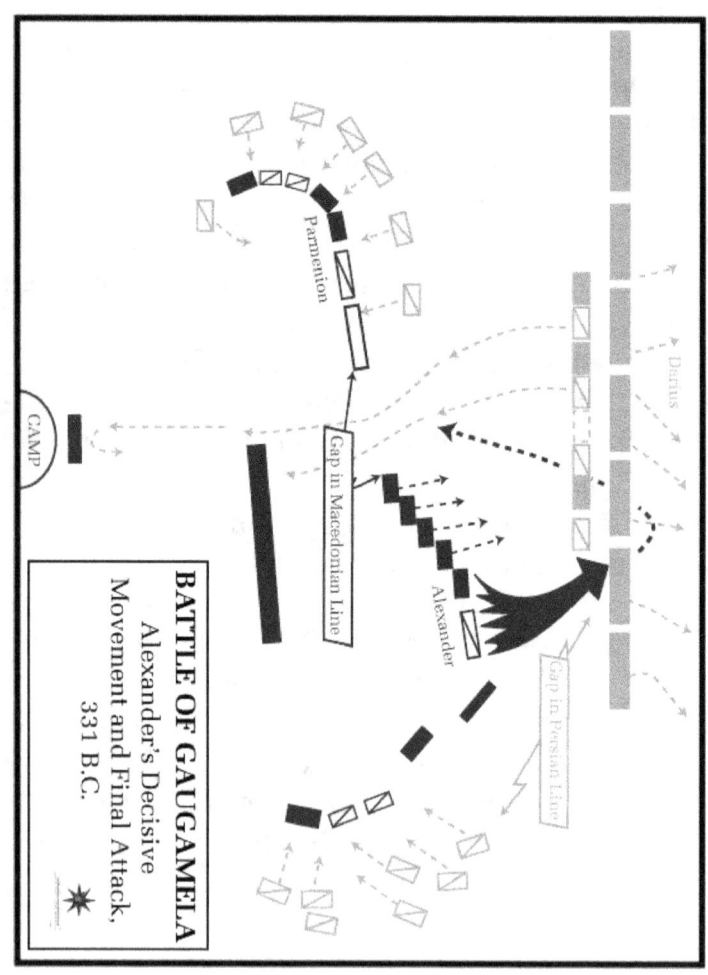

Darius, witnessing the collapse of his center and the impending defeat of his forces, made the fateful decision to flee the battlefield. Many Persians fought on, nearly overwhelming Parmenio on the Macedonian left. Nevertheless, his flight served as a crippling blow to the morale of the Persian army. Alexander turned back from his crushing maneuver and fought his way back to Parmenio. Without their king to lead them, the Persian forces lost cohesion and direction, eventually quitting the field.

In the aftermath of the battle, Alexander's gamble paid off spectacularly. His tactical brilliance and decisive maneuvering had not only secured a resounding victory against overwhelming odds but had also shattered the myth of Persian invincibility. The Battle of Gaugamela marked the climax of Alexander's conquest of the Persian Empire, cementing his status as one of history's greatest military commanders and paving the way for the expansion of his empire across the known world.

Reflecting on Triumphs

From overcoming daunting odds at the Granicus River to outmaneuvering Persian defenses at Tyre and decisively defeating Darius III at Gaugamela, Alexander's conquests exemplify the power of vision, leadership, and military innovation. Ultimately, Alexander's legacy serves as a testament to the indomitable spirit of human ambition and the enduring impact of those who dare to pursue greatness.

With the dust settling on the battlefields of Persia and the Empire reeling from the shock of Gaugamela, we take a step back. Between Issus and Gaugamela, Alexander's gaze had turned towards Egypt, a land of ancient mysteries and divine prophecies. In the midst of conquests that would prove his military genius, Egypt would offer Alexander something different: A chance to be recognized as more than a conqueror. Perhaps even as a god. The next chapter will explore how Alexander's encounter with the Oracle of Amun in the Siwa Oasis would confirm his divine status and solidify his place in history as a ruler of singular divinity.

Chapter 5: Egypt, the Oracle, and Divine Kingship

In a land where gods and kings were one, a Macedonian conqueror sought the affirmation of his divine right to rule. The sands of Egypt were not just a conquest for Alexander but a stage for the divine endorsement that would solidify his status as a ruler destined for greatness. As Alexander set his sights on the ancient land of the Nile, he was propelled both by his thirst for territorial expansion and also by the allure of Egypt's rich cultural history, its enigmatic mystique, and its revered legacy of divine rulership.

From the moment Alexander crossed into Egypt in 332 B.C.E., his journey took on a mythic quality. Legends whispered of Egypt as the birthplace of civilization, where pharaohs reigned as earthly manifestations of the gods. To conquer Egypt was to claim a realm steeped in both earthly power and celestial authority. It was a land where every stone bore witness to the divine, and every river whispered secrets of eternity.

Alexander's conquest of Egypt was a balance of diplomacy and divine symbolism. Upon his arrival, he was greeted not as a mere mortal conqueror but as a liberator, welcomed by the Egyptian priesthood, who saw in him the potential for a new era of prosperity and stability. In the grand city of Memphis, Alexander paid homage to the ancient gods, honoring their temples and rituals, while cleverly inserting himself into the pantheon of Egyptian mythology.

The Conquest of Egypt

Nestled at the crossroads of continents and civilizations, Egypt offered bountiful resources and wealth along with unparalleled strategic advantages. Its control meant dominance over the vital trade routes of the Eastern Mediterranean and access to the riches of the Nile Delta.

Egypt served as a foundation in Alexander's logistical network, providing a secure base from which to launch further campaigns into the heartland of Persia. Within the elaborate web of Alexander's campaign, Egypt emerged as a pivotal cornerstone, its importance stretching well beyond its geographical boundaries.

The Strategic Importance of Egypt

The conquest of Egypt provided several crucial advantages. Firstly, its geographic position in the northeastern corner of Africa offered a natural barrier against potential enemies coming from the south, providing a relatively secure flank for Alexander's growing empire. Egypt's control also facilitated domination over key trade routes linking the Eastern Mediterranean with the vast territories of the Persian Empire and beyond. These trade routes served as arteries of commerce, allowing for the flow of goods, resources, and intelligence crucial for sustaining and expanding Alexander's military operations.

Egypt's fertile lands, particularly the Nile Delta, served as a breadbasket for the region, ensuring a steady supply of food and provisions for Alexander's armies. The Nile River provided a reliable means of transportation, too. It enabled the swift movement of troops and supplies throughout the kingdom. This strategic positioning and logistical infrastructure transformed Egypt into a vital hub.

By consolidating control over Egypt and its coastline, Alexander effectively dismantled the Persian navy's operational bases and neutralized its ability to pose a significant threat to his ambitions. With the Eastern Mediterranean firmly under his control, Alexander could now focus his attention on expanding his empire eastward into the heartland of Persia without the looming shadow of a naval adversary.

Alexander's approach to Egypt held profound implications for cultural integration within his empire. Beyond mere conquest, his strategy encompassed a nuanced understanding of the importance of cultural and political cohesion in maintaining stability and securing long-term allegiance from conquered peoples. In Egypt, a land steeped in millennia of tradition and deeply rooted in its own distinct cultural identity, Alexander recognized the necessity of embracing and respecting local customs and beliefs.

Central to Alexander's cultural strategy in Egypt was his deference to Egyptian religion and traditions. He showed reverence for the ancient gods and rituals of Egypt. Alexander thereby endeared himself to the Egyptian populace. For a people who had languished under Persian rule for nearly two centuries, the arrival of Alexander presented a glimmer of hope and a chance for liberation from foreign oppression. His acceptance of the title of pharaoh and his anointment as the "son of the gods" in Memphis were not merely symbolic gestures. They were calculated moves to align himself with the divine lineage of Egypt's past rulers. In doing so, Alexander sought to legitimize his rule (Zhou, 2023).

Egypt's Liberator

The conquest of Egypt in 332 B.C.E. was relatively peaceful compared to some of Alexander's other military campaigns. Rather than facing significant resistance from the Egyptian people, he was largely welcomed as a liberator from the Persians. This marked a significant turning point in his campaign, showcasing his adept diplomatic approach to governance.

Recognizing the deep-seated resentment harbored by the Egyptian populace towards their Persian overlords, Alexander tactfully positioned himself not as a conqueror, but as a liberator from foreign oppression. Upon his arrival, he leveraged this sentiment to gain widespread support and loyalty among the Egyptian people.

Alexander's diplomatic finesse was evident in his interactions with the Egyptian priesthood and ruling elite. Rather than imposing Greek customs and institutions forcefully, he demonstrated respect for Egyptian religion and traditions, paying homage to the ancient gods and participating in sacred rituals.

Alexander's governance in Egypt reflected a pragmatic blend of inclusivity and efficiency. He appointed local officials to key administrative positions, allowing for the continued functioning of Egyptian institutions and ensuring a degree of continuity in governance. By incorporating Egyptian customs and practices into his administration, Alexander fostered a sense of unity and cooperation among the diverse population of Egypt, thereby mitigating the risk of widespread rebellion (Zhou, 2023).

Alexander's Coronation as Pharaoh

The ascension of Alexander the Great to the title of pharaoh of Egypt was not just a proclamation of authority. He carefully orchestrated the event to solidify his divine status among his subjects. Central to this transformation was Alexander's visit to the Oracle of Amun at Siwa, a pivotal moment that would shape his legacy and cement his claim to the throne of Egypt.

The Oracle of Amun at Siwa

The Oracle of Amun held immense significance in the ancient world as a revered sanctuary where divine wisdom was believed to be imparted. Seeking validation of his divine right to rule, Alexander embarked on a dangerous journey through the Egyptian desert to reach the sanctuary at Siwa. Upon his arrival, he underwent a sacred ritual, seeking guidance and affirmation from the god Amun himself.

The pronouncement of the Oracle at Siwa, declaring Alexander as the "son of Amun," carried profound implications for his reign in Egypt. In the eyes of his followers and subjects, this divine endorsement elevated Alexander to the status of a god-king, a mortal infused with the divine essence of Amun. By aligning himself with the highest deity in the Egyptian pantheon, Alexander not only legitimized his rule but also solidified his authority as the rightful pharaoh of Egypt (Holmes, 2022).

Alexander's anointment as the son of Amun extended far beyond mere ceremonial symbolism. It served as a powerful tool of propaganda, bolstering his divine status and enhancing his aura of invincibility in the eyes of his subjects. To the Egyptian people, Alexander was not only some foreign conqueror – he was a divine savior, destined to bring prosperity and stability to their land. Alexander's adoption of the title of pharaoh and his emulation of Egyptian religious customs further endeared him to the Egyptian people. His willingness to embrace Egyptian culture and integrate himself into the fabric of Egyptian society was as much a practical political consideration as it was a way to massage his own ego. Perhaps more.

The Temple of Amun at Siwa, seen from the north (Unger, 2001).

The Founding of Alexandria

The founding of Alexandria, a city born from the convergence of ancient prophecy and strategic foresight, illustrates the grand vision and ambition of Alexander the Great. Prophecies foretold a great city rising on the shores of Egypt, destined to become a beacon of civilization and a hub of trade and culture. Inspired by this divine decree, Alexander laid the foundation stones of Alexandria, a city that would soon emerge as one of the greatest centers of learning, commerce, and cosmopolitanism in the ancient world.

The Strategic and Symbolic Importance of Alexandria

Central to Alexander's vision for Alexandria was its role as a cultural center, where the arts, sciences, and philosophies of the ancient world would flourish. To realize this ambition, Alexander invited scholars, intellectuals, and artists from Greece, Egypt, and beyond to settle in the city, fostering an atmosphere of intellectual exchange and innovation.

Symbolically, Alexandria embodied Alexander's visionary dream of creating a cosmopolitan and culturally vibrant hub that would serve as a beacon of enlightenment and innovation. It represented the epitome of his vision for a fusion of Greek and local cultures, where diverse peoples could coexist and collaborate in pursuit of knowledge and progress.

The cultural dynamism of Alexandria became unparalleled in the ancient world. It was a melting pot of civilizations. This cultural exchange was represented by the construction of two iconic monuments after Alexander's death: the Library of Alexandria (by Ptolemy I Soter) and the Lighthouse of Alexandria (by Ptolemy II Philadelphos). The Library aimed to collect and preserve all human knowledge, becoming a symbol of Alexander's intellectual prowess and his commitment to spreading Greek culture and learning (Garlinghouse, 2022).

Alexander recognized the importance of education in cultivating a well-rounded citizenry and promoting social cohesion. In addition to its library, Alexandria boasted renowned institutions such as the Museum, which was a center for scholarly research and intellectual discourse. Here, scholars and students from all walks of life gathered to study mathematics, astronomy, medicine, and philosophy, contributing to the advancement of human knowledge and understanding.

Beyond its economic and cultural significance, Alexandria embodied Alexander's vision of cosmopolitanism. The city welcomed people of many backgrounds, languages, and beliefs. Greek, Egyptian, Persian, Jewish, and other communities coexisted harmoniously to enrich the city's social fabric and contribute to its vibrant culture and identity.

Similarly, the Lighthouse of Alexandria became one of the Seven Wonders of the Ancient World. It was a beacon (literally) of navigational excellence, guiding ships safely to Alexandria's bustling harbor. Its construction not only showcased the city's maritime power but also reflected Alexander's ambition to establish Alexandria as a preeminent center of trade and commerce in the Mediterranean. It symbolized Alexander's vision of a city that would lead human achievement and ingenuity.

Alexandria became a vital link between the Mediterranean world and the civilizations of the Near East and beyond. Its strategic location made it a coveted prize for successive empires and conquerors throughout history, from the Ptolemies and Romans to the Byzantines and Arabs. The legacy of Alexandria's strategic importance endures to this day, as it continues to be a thriving metropolis and a center of trade, culture, and scholarship in the modern world.

Alexandria's Impact on World History

Alexandria's importance transcended the boundaries of Alexander's empire, leaving a lasting mark on world history that resonates to this day. As a center of learning and cultural exchange, the city played a pivotal role in shaping the course of human civilization, attracting scholars and intellectuals from across the ancient world.

2nd century C.E. Roman coins minted in Alexandria and depicting the famous lighthouse, or *Pharos* (Ginolerhino, 2006).

The Library of Alexandria was a crucible of intellectual inquiry. There were groundbreaking advances in fields like mathematics, astronomy, medicine, and philosophy. Scholars such as Euclid, Archimedes, and Eratosthenes made significant contributions to human knowledge within the walls of the library, laying the foundations for scientific and philosophical inquiry that shaped the course of history for centuries to come (Garlinghouse, 2022).

However, Alexandria's legacy is also marked by tragedy. The loss of the Library of Alexandria, whether through fire, conquest, or neglect, is often mourned as one of the greatest cultural losses in history. The destruction of countless priceless manuscripts and scrolls represents a profound setback for human knowledge, depriving future generations of insights into the ancient world and its achievements. Nevertheless, the spirit of Alexandria endures, as scholars and historians continue to uncover fragments of its lost treasures and seek to preserve and celebrate its rich cultural heritage.

Gateway to the East

In the wake of Alexander's conquest of Egypt, the landscape of his empire underwent a transformative shift. With Egypt firmly under his control and his rule endorsed by divine pronouncements, Alexander stood poised at the threshold of unparalleled greatness. The acquisition of Egypt expanded his territorial reach and solidified his status as a ruler destined for legendary distinction. Through his adept diplomacy and willingness to embrace local customs, Alexander successfully integrated himself into the fabric of Egyptian society, laying the groundwork for a stable and prosperous reign.

Yet, Alexander's ambitions were far from satisfied. Beyond the borders of Egypt lay vast territories teeming with untold riches and formidable challenges. The lure of the unknown beckoned to him, igniting a fire within his soul that drove him ever onward in pursuit of glory and conquest. Thus, as we bid farewell to the sands of Egypt, we embark on a new chapter in Alexander's epic saga—the daring campaigns in India.

In the next chapter, we will journey with Alexander as he leads his armies into the heart of Asia, where the lush valleys and towering mountains of the Indian subcontinent await. Here, amidst the rich heritage of Indian civilization and the myriad kingdoms that dot the landscape, Alexander's determination will be tested as never before. From the fierce battles against powerful adversaries to encounters with the wisdom of ancient sages, Alexander's quest for glory will persevere through its most formidable obstacles and profound lessons.

Chapter 6: To the Edge of the Known World

Venturing into lands no Macedonian had seen before, Alexander transcended the role of conqueror, emerging instead as a curious explorer navigating a world of astonishing wonder. The Indian Campaign embodied a transformative journey that tested his ambition, the expanse of his tolerance, and the loyalty of his stalwart Macedonian countrymen.

The Campaign in India: The Battle of the Hydaspes

The Indian Campaign undertaken by Alexander the Great held immense strategic importance, both in terms of territorial expansion and cultural exchange. India represented a gateway to (allegedly) vast wealth and untapped resources, including spices, textiles, and precious metals. Control over these resources promised to enrich Alexander's empire and solidify his dominance in the ancient world. India's geographical position at the crossroads of trade routes connecting East and West made it a coveted prize for any ambitious conqueror (*Alexander's Crossing of the Hindu Kush and His Campaigns in India*, 2023).

The Battle of the Hydaspes is yet another witness to Alexander's prowess and strategic brilliance. Set against the backdrop of the mighty Hydaspes River in 326 B.C.E., this confrontation between the forces of Alexander and King Porus of the Paurava kingdom encapsulates the culmination of Alexander's Indian Campaign.

The battle was fought along the banks of the Hydaspes River (modern-day Jhelum River), serves as a pivotal moment in Alexander's Indian Campaign. Here, Alexander faced King Porus in a confrontation that tested the tenacity of his troops and the depth of his strategic ingenuity. The outcome of this battle determined the fate of the region and shaped the course of Alexander's conquests and legacy (Raikar, n.d.).

King Porus: A New and Powerful Adversary

King Porus of the Pauravas was a formidable opponent to Alexander the Great, particularly during the Battle of Hydaspes. His decision to confront Alexander rather than yield to his authority showcased his courage, strategic acumen, and determination to defend his realm against foreign invaders (*Porus*, 2002).

One of King Porus' most notable strengths lay in the composition and organization of his army. Despite being numerically inferior to the Macedonian forces, Porus' army was well-equipped and disciplined, comprising a mix of infantry, cavalry, and, most notably, war elephants. These massive beasts were trained for battle and adorned with armor, presenting a mighty challenge to Alexander's renowned cavalry and infantry tactics.

The inclusion of war elephants in Porus' army significantly altered the dynamics of the battlefield. These towering creatures instilled fear and confusion among Alexander's troops, who had little experience facing such opponents. The sheer size and strength of the elephants made them difficult to confront directly, forcing Alexander to adapt his tactics and devise new strategies to counter their threat.

King Porus' leadership played a crucial role in bolstering the morale and cohesion of his troops. His reputation as a brave and capable commander inspired loyalty and dedication among his soldiers, who fought with unwavering determination under his command. His ability to instill confidence in his men and lead them into battle with conviction further enhanced his effectiveness as a military leader.

In addition to his military prowess, King Porus demonstrated strategic foresight and resourcefulness in his approach to the conflict with Alexander. By choosing to engage the Macedonian forces at the Hydaspes River, Porus sought to exploit the natural advantages afforded by the river and the capabilities of his army to maximize his chances of success.

The Battle

As the swollen Hydaspes River surged with rain and melting snow, it became a formidable natural barrier. Facing off against Porus' well-equipped and disciplined army, estimated to be between 30,000 to 50,000 strong, Alexander's forces, roughly 40,000 in number, encountered a worthy opponent bolstered by chariots and the fearsome war elephants of the Indian subcontinent (Wasson, 2014).

Despite these obstacles, Alexander's tactical adaptability shone through in his response to the challenges presented by Porus' army and the adverse weather conditions he faced. Recognizing that it would be impossible to cross the river into the teeth of the enemy, as he had done at Issus and the Granicus, Alexander knew he needed to cross a large portion of his army unmarked by the enemy. He established a large camp on his side of the river, from where he would march his troops up and down the bank, forcing Porus to deploy his own men to prevent any crossing. Eventually, the attention of the Indian king wavered when Alexander's troops persisted in their maneuvers, never seeking to cross. That's when Alexander executed his plan.

Under the cover of a stormy night, Alexander led a large portion of his army to a crossing 17 miles upstream of the camp leaving several contingents along the way who were to cross after Alexander gained a foothold on the other side. Craterus, the captain in charge of the Macedonian camp, was under orders to make it look like he was about to force a crossing, keeping Porus' attention away from anything else. Moreover, once Porus realized he had been outmaneuvered and moved to intercept

Alexander, Craterus was to cross and take the Indian army from behind.

Alexander and his men emerged cold, wet, and exhausted on the other side, still with a battle to fight. And the ruse had only partially worked. Either through spies or treachery, Porus had learned of the distant crossing and sent his son (also named Porus) to contest it with a force of chariots. It met with Alexander and his cavalry, who had pressed on ahead of the slow-moving phalanx. Without even forming up, Alexander charged the enemy chariots, many of which became stuck in the mud formed in the overnight storm. Young Porus was killed, and his father soon learned that a large Macedonian force was bearing down on him.

Once across the Hydaspes, and through the advance chariot force, Alexander faced the task of neutralizing the war elephants. Concentrating his attacks on the flanks and employing the long sarissas of his Macedonian phalangites, Alexander's troops proved adept at repelling the formidable beasts, though they took heavy losses. This tactical adaptation showcased Alexander's ability to identify and exploit his adversaries' weaknesses, even in the face of seemingly insurmountable odds.

Surrounded by the chaos and carnage of battle, Alexander's respect for King Porus and the valiant defense of his realm became increasingly apparent. Despite being on opposing sides of the conflict, Alexander admired his courage and determination,

Alexander's night crossing of the Hydaspes River
(Martini & Department of History, United States Military Academy, 2006).

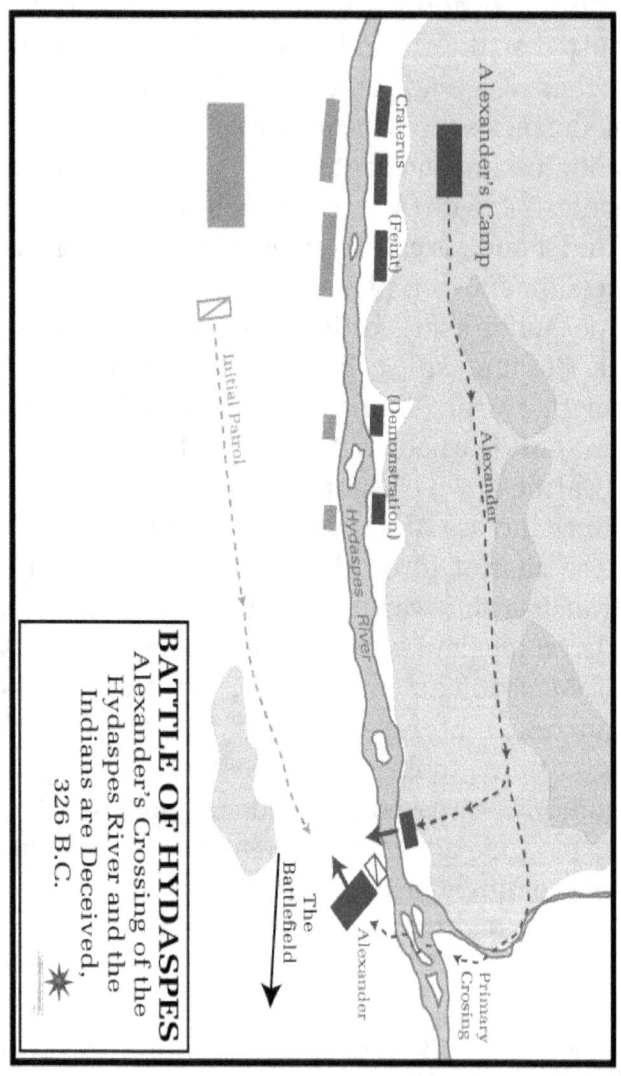

recognizing in him a worthy adversary deserving of respect. Indeed, the Indian king cut a dashing figure, clad in mail and riding his largest elephant into the battle.

But Alexander could not be stopped. The phalanx pinned Porus' infantry in place, while the Companions and other cavalry formations from across Alexander's empire drove off the Indian horse. The battle was fierce, and Bucephalus (now almost 30 years old) was either killed under Alexander or succumbed to his wounds shortly after the battle. Regardless, the Macedonian king was victorious, and the Indian army eventually broke. Craterus crossed with the rest of the army to pursue the enemy.

Alexander's admiration of Porus seemed to be genuine. Indeed, made Porus a satrap of his empire, allowing him to govern the land he had always governed. He even increased the Indian king's holdings (*Porus*, 2002). This respect for Porus' valor exemplifies Alexander's ability to transcend the boundaries of conquest and acknowledge the strength of his adversaries, a trait that earned him the loyalty and admiration of both friend and foe.

Encounters With New Cultures

From the bustling cities of the Indus Valley to the plains of the Punjab, Alexander's encounters with the different cultures of India left a lasting mark on his psyche. His insatiable curiosity led him to engage with local leaders, scholars, and artisans, seeking to unravel the mysteries of these ancient civilizations and forge connections beyond the battlefield.

Surrounded by vibrant Indian culture, Alexander displayed a remarkable willingness to embrace new ideas and traditions. He immersed himself in the customs and rituals of the people he encountered, gaining insights into their beliefs, governance systems, and social structures. From the teachings of Indian philosophers to the craftsmanship of local artisans, Alexander's thirst for knowledge knew no bounds.

Cultural Exchange and Integration

Bilingual silver tetradrachm of the Indo-Greek king Antialkidas, ruler of Taxila, Punjab (late 2nd century B.C.E.). Obverse: Antialkidas wearing the Greek aegis and holding a spear. Greek legend: BASILEOS NIKEPHOROU ANTIALKIDOU "Of the victorious king, Antialkidas." Reverse: Zeus with lotus scepter backed by Nike riding an elephant. Karoshti legend: MAHARAJASA JAYADHARASA ANTIALIKITASA "Victorious king Antialkidas" (Classical Numismatic Group, 2022). Another artefact from the period, the Heliodorus Pillar, suggests Antialkidas may have been a devotee of the Hindu god Vishnu.

The cultural exchange and integration that occurred during Alexander's expedition into India represented a meeting of civilizations. This period witnessed a dynamic interchange between Greek and Indian cultures, leading to a synthesis of artistic, intellectual, and social traditions that enriched both societies. It offered a sharp contrast to the fierce bloodshed of Alexander's battles.

One of the most significant outcomes of this cultural exchange was the establishment of Greek colonies in various parts of the Indian subcontinent. These colonies served as centers of cultural interaction, where Greek settlers mingled with local populations, exchanging ideas, languages, and customs. Greek architecture, art, and urban planning influenced the development of Indian cities, while Indian textiles, spices, and artistic motifs found their way into Greek markets.

Indo-Greek art, characterized by its synthesis of Greek and Indian artistic styles, emerged as a distinctive expression of this cultural fusion. Greek sculptural techniques influenced the depiction of Indian deities and mythological figures, while Indian motifs and iconography found expression in Greek art forms (Sanujit, 2011).

The encounter between Greek and Indian cultures allowed a deeper understanding and appreciation of each other's religious beliefs and practices. Greek travelers and historians documented Indian religious rituals, mythologies, and spiritual practices, while Indian texts and teachings influenced Greek interpretations of religion and spirituality. This cross-cultural exchange fostered a spirit of pluralism, with both populations merging into a new cultural identity.

Philosophical and Scientific Impressions

In India, Alexander encountered a rich philosophical tradition that left a lasting impression on him (Arrian, *Anabasis* 7.1-3). Indian philosophers, known as sages or rishis, were esteemed advisors to the kings and princes of India, offering insights into matters of governance, ethics, and spirituality. Alexander was struck by the depth and complexity of Indian philosophical thought, which encompassed a wide range of schools of philosophy, including Vedanta, Samkhya, Nyaya, and Yoga (*Schools of Indian Philosophy*, n.d.).

One aspect of Indian philosophy that impressed Alexander was its emphasis on spiritual liberation and the pursuit of inner wisdom. Indian philosophers explored profound questions about the nature of existence, the self, and the universe, seeking to go beyond the limitations of material reality and attain spiritual enlightenment. This focus on inner transformation and self-realization resonated deeply with Alexander, who had himself been engaged in philosophical inquiries into the nature of reality and the meaning of life since his time with Aristotle.

Indian philosophers were renowned for their ethical teachings and moral wisdom. The concept of *dharma*, or righteous conduct, was central to Indian philosophical thought. It emphasized the importance of living a virtuous and ethical life under one's duty and social role. Alexander admired the ethical clarity and practical wisdom of Indian philosophical teachings.

Indian philosophical traditions also placed a strong emphasis on logic and rational inquiry. Schools of Indian philosophy such as Nyaya developed sophisticated systems of logical reasoning and argumentation, which impressed Alexander with their rigor and precision. He recognized a shared commitment to rational inquiry between the Greek and Indian cultures.

Alexander was also deeply impressed by the strength of Indian medical science, which many considered to be more advanced than Macedonia's. The Indian medical tradition, rooted in ancient texts such as the Ayurveda, had developed a comprehensive understanding of the human body, illnesses, and treatment methods.

One area that particularly fascinated him was the Indian knowledge of herbal remedies. Indian physicians had compiled extensive guides detailing the properties and uses of medicinal plants. These herbal remedies were often administered in complex formulations tailored to the specific needs of individual patients. The effectiveness of these herbal medicines was evident in their ability to treat a wide range of ailments, from fevers and digestive disorders to more serious conditions such as infections and injuries.

Indian medical practitioners had also developed sophisticated surgical techniques that were far ahead of their time. Indian texts such as the *Sushruta Samhita* detailed surgical procedures, including plastic surgery, cataract surgery, and even techniques for repairing fractures and dislocations. The detailed descriptions found in these texts attest to the skill and precision of ancient Indian surgeons, who were able to perform complex surgeries with remarkable success rates.

Dietary Influences

The cultural exchange between Greece and India extended to culinary traditions, too. The result was a rich fusion of flavors and gastronomic influences that left a lasting imprint on both societies. The introduction of Indian dietary practices and ingredients to Greece, and vice versa, led to the diversification and enrichment of Greek cuisine, transforming culinary landscapes on both sides of the ancient world (Monzani, 2025).

One notable influence of Indian cuisine on Greek food was the spread of vegetarianism. In India, vegetarianism was a longstanding dietary practice deeply rooted in religious and cultural traditions. As Greek travelers and traders encountered Indian culinary customs, they were exposed to a wide variety of vegetarian dishes and cooking techniques. Many

Greeks were inspired by the new flavors and supposed nutritional benefits of vegetarian cuisine (Monzani, 2025).

Indian ingredients such as yogurt and ghee found their way into Greek cooking, adding new dimensions of flavor and texture to Greek recipes. Yogurt became a staple ingredient in Greek cuisine, used in sauces, dressings, and marinades. Ghee, a clarified butter widely used in Indian cooking, was embraced by Greek bakers and chefs for its rich, nutty flavor and versatility in baking and frying.

An example of the fusion between Greek and Indian culinary traditions is the similarity between Indian *naan* and Greek *pita* bread. Both naan and pita are flatbreads made from a simple dough of flour, water, and yeast, which is then baked in a hot oven until golden brown and puffed up. The use of yogurt in naan dough, a common practice in Indian cooking, mirrors the Greek tradition of incorporating yogurt into bread recipes.

Spiritual and Religious Exchanges

Following Alexander's death, Greece is believed to have become an importer of Buddhism to the West. This suggests that the encounters between Greek and Indian cultures during Alexander's campaigns facilitated the spread of Buddhist teachings and practices to the Mediterranean region. Greek merchants, travelers, and scholars journeyed to India in the wake of Alexander's conquests would have encountered Buddhist communities and teachings, which they subsequently brought back to Greece.

A significant outcome of this cultural exchange was the adoption of practices like meditation and yoga into the daily lives of people in the regions under Alexander's influence. The practice of meditation, in particular, was popular among Greek philosophers and intellectuals, who were drawn to its contemplative and introspective nature. Similarly, yoga, with its emphasis on physical and spiritual discipline, appealed to individuals seeking inner harmony and self-realization.

The cultural interactions during Alexander's campaigns are believed to have led to the creation of the first representations of Buddha in statue form. Greek sculptors, inspired by the artistic traditions of India, began to depict Buddha in a manner that combined Greek artistic techniques with Indian iconography. These early representations of Buddha, known as Greco-Buddhist art, showcase the fusion of Greek and Indian artistic traditions and attest to the cultural exchange that occurred during this period (Vasiloudis, 2024).

Recognition of Alexander in Indian Culture

The recognition of Alexander in Indian culture is a fascinating aspect of the historical and cultural exchange between India and the Western world. In ancient Indian literature, Alexander was often mentioned under the name *Skanda*, becoming associated with the Indian war god of the same name (Pillai, 1937). This association reflects the impact that Alexander's campaigns had on Indian civilization, as well as the lasting impression he left on the cultural and religious landscape of the region.

The name Skanda, derived from ancient Sanskrit, carries significant meaning in Indian tradition. It translates to "the leader of an army," emphasizing Alexander's role as a renowned military commander and conqueror. When it incorporated Alexander into the pantheon of Indian deities, Indian literature acknowledged his expertise as a warrior and his influence on the course of history.

The association of Alexander with Skanda emphasizes the extent to which his exploits were woven into the cultural and religious fabric of ancient India. Through conquest and cultural exchange, Alexander's campaigns left a long-lasting mark on Indian civilization, shaping its literary, artistic, and religious traditions for centuries to come. The inclusion of Alexander in Indian mythology reflects the adaptability of Indian culture, which has a long history of incorporating foreign influences into its beliefs and traditions.

The Challenge of Governing a Diverse Empire

As Alexander's empire expanded across vast territories, he faced a multitude of logistical, administrative, and cultural challenges that tested the limits of his leadership and adaptability.

Logistical, Administrative, and Cultural Challenges

Alexander had to ensure the efficient transportation of troops, supplies, and resources across long distances, often in harsh and unfamiliar terrain. Maintaining communication and coordination between distant regions posed logistical hurdles, and it required the establishment of efficient communication networks and logistical infrastructure like roads and bridges (Kings and Generals, 2018).

Administratively, governing a diverse and multicultural empire required effective administrative systems and policies. Alexander had to navigate the complexities of governing regions with diverse languages, cultures, and traditions, often relying on a combination of local administrators and Macedonian officials to maintain stability and order. The integration of conquered territories into the empire's administrative framework required standardized laws, taxation systems, and bureaucratic institutions (*Alexander the Great's Vision for an Empire: Governance and Administration*, 2023).

Culturally, Alexander faced the challenge of reconciling the customs, religions, and beliefs of the peoples he conquered with those of the Macedonian ruling class. He adopted a policy of cultural assimilation and encouraged the spread of the Greek language and institutions throughout the empire while adopting certain aspects of the cultures he conquered. However, this policy also led to tensions with his Macedonian nobility and resistance from local populations who sought to preserve their cultural identity and autonomy (Walbank, 2025).

Diplomacy at Work

Alexander employed several strategies to govern the territories under his rule, seeking to balance centralized Greek control with local autonomy.

To govern the vast territories of his empire, Alexander followed the Persians in appointing local satraps, or provincial governors, to administer regions according to local customs and traditions. While maintaining overall control, Alexander delegated authority to trusted individuals from various ethnic backgrounds, including Persians, Greeks, Egyptians, and Indians, to govern their respective regions. This decentralized system allowed for greater flexibility in governance and facilitated the administration of different populations *(Alexander the Great's vision for an empire: Governance and administration. 2023).*

Alexander's army was composed of soldiers from various ethnic backgrounds, including Macedonians, Greeks, Persians, Bactrians, Indians, and other conquered peoples. To foster loyalty and cohesion within his military forces, Alexander integrated local troops into his army and offered them opportunities for advancement and recognition (Wasson, 2023).

Uniting Worlds Through Conquest

Alexander's expedition into India represented the culmination of his ambitious conquests and was a testament to his ability to navigate the complexities of governance and cultural integration. As he ventured further into the Indian subcontinent, Alexander faced unprecedented challenges that tested the limits of his leadership and adaptability. Yet, he rose to the occasion, demonstrating both military prowess on the battlefield and diplomatic finesse in his efforts to govern and unite many peoples.

Throughout his Indian campaign, Alexander employed a range of strategies to consolidate his rule, from marriage alliances to the appointment of local satraps and the integration of diverse troops into his army. His encounters with Indian societies fostered a rich exchange of ideas, beliefs, and practices, leaving a lasting imprint on both Greek and Indian cultures.

As we further explore the essence of Alexander's leadership, it becomes evident that he was not just a conqueror, but a visionary leader who sought to bridge the divide between East and West. His ambitions went beyond conquest as he aspired to create an empire that straddled worlds, uniting many peoples under a common banner. It is through the exploration of Alexander's character as both a warrior and a king that we gain deeper insights into the complexities of his legacy and the enduring impact of his achievements on the course of history.

Chapter 7: The Warrior and the King

Alexander's name is synonymous with conquest, ambition, and empire building. Born in the turbulent landscape of ancient Macedonia, he emerged as a force to be reckoned with—a prodigious military strategist whose tactics continue to inspire scholars and commanders alike. But beyond his prowess on the battlefield, Alexander's reign showcases the power of diplomacy and cultural exchange. Unlike many conquerors of his time, Alexander sought not only to subjugate but also to assimilate, embracing the customs and traditions of the lands he conquered in a bid for unity. His empire was a patchwork of Greek, Persian, Egyptian, Indian, and many other cultures that stood as a testament to his vision of a harmonious and interconnected world.

As we journey through the pages of history, we unravel the complex layers of Alexander's character. He was not merely a warrior-king, but an individual driven by an insatiable thirst for knowledge, glory, and the pursuit of greatness. His relationships played a pivotal role in shaping his rule and defining his legacy. From his lifelong friendship with Hephaestion to his tumultuous relationship with his father, Philip II, Alexander's connections offer a window into the motivations and machinations of a ruler whose ambitions knew no bounds. Woven throughout his life are the threads of myth and legend, each embellishment adding to the allure and mystique of a man whose name would echo through the ages.

Alexander's Military Genius and Innovations

Building on the revolutionary military system established by Philip II, Alexander the Great inherited a force that was already professional, highly integrated, and formidable. Yet his true genius lay in transforming this solid foundation into a dynamic and multi-dimensional instrument of conquest. Rather than simply using what he inherited, Alexander refined and expanded its capabilities to address the varied and complex challenges of his campaigns. His innovations spanned tactical flexibility, cavalry operations, siege warfare, logistics, intelligence, and even psychological warfare.

Tactical Innovations

While Philip's legacy of the sarissa-armed phalanx remained the backbone of his army, Alexander reimagined its role on the battlefield. No longer a static force committed solely to frontal assaults, the phalanx under Alexander became a flexible "anvil" that fixed enemy formations in place. He would subtly adjust the formation's depth, spacing, and orientation in real-time to create exploitable gaps in enemy lines. This adaptability was critical in battles like Gaugamela, where coordinated maneuvers allowed his cavalry to penetrate the enemy's flanks and decisively disrupt their cohesion.

However, although the dense Macedonian phalanx was nearly invulnerable to a frontal assault, it was slow to maneuver and extremely vulnerable on its flanks. In keeping with Philip's combined arms approach, Alexander placed a battalion of *hypaspists* next to the phalangites. There is some debate among scholars, but it seems these elite troops were heavily armed in the manner of Greek hoplites from the previous century. In close order, the hypaspists could still withstand incredible punishment because of their armament. But, counterintuitively, their heavier armor, larger shields, and shorter spears meant that individuals were better protected and could operate more independently. They could deploy and redeploy more quickly to offer steady defense or devastating assaults wherever necessary – and Alexander employed them masterfully

Building on the elite Companion cavalry established by his father, Alexander elevated their function to a decisive and innovative role. He personally led these highly trained units in rapid, penetrating shock charges that could dismantle larger enemy formations. The phalanx held enemy forces in place while the cavalry acted as the "hammer" to its "anvil," charging the flanks and rear of the enemy who were pinned in place. In addition to these heavy cavalry charges, Alexander diversified his cavalry deployments with lighter, more agile horsemen for reconnaissance and skirmishing. He would often pair them with light infantry and skirmishers (as at Gaugamela) to offer a screen behind which the light horse could rest and reform. His light cavalry could ensure constant pressure and flexibility across the battlefield (Historia Civilis, 2017).

However, Alexander's ingenuity was not confined to open-field engagements. Confronted with heavily fortified cities, he pioneered advanced siege techniques that combined engineering brilliance with tactical daring. At the Siege of Tyre in 332 B.C.E., for example, his causeway gap to the (previously thought) impregnable island eventually neutralized the city's naval defenses. His engineers also refined the use of siege towers, battering rams, and early artillery devices like catapults and ballistae. This meant his forces could breach walls with reduced casualties. These innovations secured vital victories and established siegecraft methods that would influence military engineering for centuries (Hughes, 2023).

Advancements in Grand Strategy

Alexander understood that sustaining long, far-reaching campaigns required more than battlefield prowess; it demanded superior logistics and information gathering. He revolutionized the traditional supply system by establishing flexible, responsive supply lines and strategically located depots. These innovations ensured that his rapidly advancing forces remained well-provisioned, even in hostile and unfamiliar terrain. Complementing these logistical advances was an extensive network of scouts and intelligence agents. They often gathered real-time data on enemy movements, terrain features, and potential weak points. Through them, Alexander was able to adjust his tactics swiftly and accurately, often pre-empting enemy actions and turning the tide of battle before it even started.

In aid of this, Alexander's innovations extended into the psychological realm, where his personal courage and charismatic leadership served as potent weapons. His fearless presence on the battlefield inspired his troops and sapped the morale of his adversaries before the fighting began. Moreover, Alexander adeptly employed psychological tactics—ranging from the use of strategic propaganda to deliberate displays of power—that sowed doubt and fear among enemy. Off the battlefield, his willingness to integrate soldiers from conquered territories and to adopt elements of local customs helped to consolidate his empire, reduce resistance, and foster unity within his ranks.

Alexander the Great's strategic innovations, therefore, went far beyond the solid military foundations laid by Philip II. Alexander completely reshaped the art of war by dynamically adapting the phalanx, revolutionizing cavalry tactics, pioneering sophisticated siege warfare, enhancing logistical and intelligence frameworks, and employing powerful psychological strategies. His multifaceted approach secured his legendary conquests, yet they also left an enduring legacy that has influenced military strategy for millennia since.

The Adoption of Persian Customs

Alexander's adoption of Persian customs and attire represented a major departure from the norms of his Macedonian upbringing, yet it may have been a calculated and strategic decision driven by a combination of factors. Scholars will continue to debate Alexander's motives. Did he buy into the eastern phenomenon of divine kingship? Was he merely a cold pragmatist trying to keep everything together? It was likely a mix of practicality and admiration, though certainty will never be possible.

Practical vs. Fascination

The debate over whether Alexander's adoption of Persian customs was a strategic move to assimilate and pacify conquered peoples or was borne from a genuine respect and fascination for Persian culture is complex and well-trodden. It involves interpreting historical evidence and understanding the motivations behind Alexander's actions, a dubious experiment at best.

On the one hand, supporters of the strategic assimilation theory argue that Alexander's adoption of Persian customs was a calculated move to consolidate power and maintain control over his empire. He embraced Persian culture and traditions to win the loyalty and support of the Persian elite and aristocracy, thereby facilitating the process of governance and pacification (and potentially alienating his Macedonians). This strategic assimilation allowed Alexander to present himself as a legitimate successor to the Persian kings. Moreover, it helped integrate Persian administrative practices and court protocols to streamline governance and promote stability within the empire (Foster, 2005).

On the other hand, advocates of the genuine respect and fascination theory claim that Alexander's adoption of Persian customs was motivated by a sincere admiration for Persian culture and civilization. Throughout his campaigns, Alexander developed a deep appreciation for the richness and sophistication of Persian society. This genuine respect for Persian culture may have influenced Alexander's decision to embrace Persian customs, as he sought to enrich his cultural horizons and understand the perspectives of his conquered subjects. Furthermore, Alexander's interactions with Persian scholars, philosophers, and artists suggest a genuine interest in learning from and engaging with Persian culture, rather than simply exploiting it for political gain. Finally, the eastern tradition of divine kingship may have held particular weight, given his prophetic birth and divine lineage (Olbrycht, 2014).

The debate over whether Alexander's adoption of Persian customs was strategic assimilation or genuine respect is likely a combination of both factors. While political considerations undoubtedly played a role in Alexander's decision-making, his genuine fascination with Persian culture and his desire to foster unity and stability within his empire likely influenced his embrace of Persian customs, as well. The complex interplay between political strategy and personal conviction makes it challenging to definitively determine the primary motivation behind Alexander's actions.

Proskynesis *and the Susa Weddings*

Regardless of where one stands on the debate between practicality and fascination, there are two episodes that illustrate the effects of Alexander's "Persianizing" tendency. In the summer of 327 B.C.E., Alexander had just completed his conquest of Persia and was about to continue into India. As a way to placate the Persians whom he had accepted into his royal court, he adopted the custom of *proskynesis* – ritual prostration before a king or deity.

The custom had a long history among the Persian nobility, but the Macedonians found the ritual grossly inappropriate. While they could tolerate his desire to wear Persian dress, Macedonians and Greeks saw ritual prostration degrading and slavish, unless performed exclusively for the gods. Divine kingship was not a Greek ideal. After the initial blowback, Alexander did not insist on the practice for his Macedonians (*Proskynesis*, 1998).

In 324, after returning to Persia from India, Alexander arrived at Susa, the eastern capital of the old Persian Empire. There, he ordered his Macedonians to take noble Persian wives. There were over 80 weddings, and Alexander himself married Stateira, the daughter of Darius. Alexander intended for the weddings to further legitimize his rule among the Persians – the children of these marriages would symbolize the union of Greece and Persia after centuries of antagonism.

His plan was at least partially successful. Although many modern scholars have suggested that the Macedonians divorced their Persian spouses after Alexander's death, there is no ancient evidence to suggest it. None. Such a reversal of Alexander's arrangement would likely have left some historical trace, given the Macedonians had nothing to gain and (perhaps) land and wealth to lose by refusing their Persian wives; moreover, the Macedonian nobility were no strangers to polygamy (Van Oppen, 2014). It's possible that the Susa Weddings did much to help Greek culture take root throughout the Near East by ensuring a strong Greek presence in the local nobility for the next several generations.

Relationships With Friends, Foes, and Love Interests

Alexander's relationships with key figures and romantic interests are intertwined with the conquests that earned him a place in history. From the steadfast companionship of Hephaestion to the encounters with Darius III and the complexities of romance with Roxana and Barsine, Alexander's relationships offer a glimpse into the man behind the legendary conqueror.

Alexander was married at least three times (Hays, 2024). His marriages had significant strategic, political, cultural, and personal implications that shaped both his reign and his legacy. Alexander's personal life was also marked by his close friendships with men. It is possible he had an intimate relationship with his friend Hephaestion, as well as with Bagoas, a young Persian dancer. The evidence for such dalliances is uncertain, and most of the scholarly arguments (for or against) concern themselves more with the preoccupations of modern scholars than genuine academic rigor.

Hephaestion: Alexander's Closest Companion

The relationship between Alexander and Hephaestion was exceedingly strong. From their formative years as companions and students under the tutelage of Aristotle to their roles as trusted comrades on the battlefield, Hephaestion was Alexander's steadfast confidant and loyal ally.

Alexander's relationship with Hephaestion exerted a profound influence on his decisions, leadership style, and the trajectory of his military campaigns. Hephaestion played a pivotal role in shaping Alexander's character and worldview, leaving an indelible mark on his reign as a leader (Stoogenke, 2024).

Alexander (Left) and Hephaestion (Right) (Neilwiththedeal, 2006).

Hephaestion served as Alexander's constant source of emotional support and counsel. Their deep bond provided Alexander with a trusted sounding board for his ideas and a sympathetic ear for his concerns. Hephaestion's presence offered Alexander a sense of companionship and camaraderie during the rigors of military conquest, bolstering his confidence and resolve in the face of the many challenges he faced.

Hephaestion surely played a significant role in shaping Alexander's strategic decisions and military tactics. As a capable commander in his own right, Hephaestion provided valuable insights and perspectives to Alexander's deliberations, helping to refine his strategies and anticipate his adversaries' moves. Their close collaboration on the battlefield enabled Alexander to adapt quickly to changing circumstances and outmaneuver his opponents, ultimately aiding his string of triumphs across Asia (*Hephaestion*, n.d.).

Hephaestion's presence exerted a moderating influence on Alexander's impulsive tendencies, tempering his boldness with caution and pragmatism. While Alexander was renowned for his boldness and willingness to take risks, Hephaestion's steadying influence helped to prevent recklessness and ensure that Alexander's decisions were grounded in reasoned judgment.

Roxana: The Most Beautiful Woman in Asia

The relationship between Alexander and Roxana, the daughter of the Bactrian noble Oxyartes, was a union marked by both political significance and personal affection. Known as one of the most beautiful women in Asia, Roxana captured Alexander's heart, leading to a marriage that blended political strategy with what appears to be genuine mutual attraction.

Roxana brought both her beauty and lineage too the union, which served to strengthen Alexander's ties to the Bactrian aristocracy. This marriage was emblematic of Alexander's efforts to integrate many cultures into his empire for the sake of unity and cooperation among his diverse subjects.

Roxana's presence by Alexander's side likely provided him with emotional support and companionship during his grueling later campaigns. Amidst the challenges of his military efforts and governance of the empire, Roxana may have served as a stabilizing influence on Alexander, offering him a sense of grounding despite the chaos of empire-building.

Alexander's relationship with Roxana may have also influenced his diplomatic decisions and interactions with native elites. By marrying Roxana, Alexander sought to bridge the divide between Macedonian and Eastern cultures, demonstrating his willingness to embrace foreign customs and traditions. This gesture likely facilitated negotiations and alliances with the local nobility, helping to consolidate Alexander's control over his vast empire.

It's important to note that the historical records provide limited insight into the specifics of Alexander and Roxana's relationship. Regardless, it is clear that Roxana's presence in Alexander's life had implications for his leadership and the course of his campaigns, contributing to his legacy as a conqueror and statesman (Fisher, n.d.).

Darius III: A Royal Rival

The rivalry between Alexander and the Persian emperor Darius III was a central narrative throughout Alexander's early campaigns. Their confrontations on the battlefield, most notably at Issus and Gaugamela, went beyond clashes of armies; they were symbolic showdowns between two towering figures of antiquity.

Darius III fueled Alexander's ambition and determination to assert his dominance over the Persian Empire. From the outset of his campaign, Alexander viewed Darius as a formidable adversary and a symbol of Persian power. This rivalry catalyzed Alexander's relentless pursuit of conquest, spurring him to push his armies to the limits and achieve ever-greater feats of military prowess (Roos, 2023).

Alexander's leadership style was greatly influenced by his rivalry with Darius III, instilling a sense of urgency and decisiveness. Faced with the impressive might of the Persian Empire, Alexander adopted a bold approach to warfare, characterized by rapid marches, daring maneuvers, and tactical gambits. His confrontations with Darius III served as crucibles of leadership, testing Alexander's resolve and forcing him to make split-second decisions in the heat of battle.

The rivalry with Darius III shaped the overall course of Alexander's campaigns, dictating the direction and focus of his military efforts. Each encounter with Darius III represented a pivotal moment in Alexander's conquests, with the outcome of these battles carrying implications for the balance of power in the ancient world. Darius drove Alexander to pursue his conquests deep into the heart of the Persian Empire, culminating in his decisive victory at the Battle of Gaugamela and the downfall of the Achaemenid Dynasty (De Santis, 2001).

Detail of Darius III from the Alexander Mosaic (Raddato, 2014).

Parysatis and Other Love Interests

Parysatis was the widow of a Persian noble. She is depicted as having captured Alexander's attention with her beauty and intellect, particularly her knowledge of Greek literature. Their relationship is often portrayed as a brief yet passionate affair, although its historical accuracy remains a subject of debate among scholars. Regardless, Parysatis' association with Alexander showcases the cultural and social mingling that characterized his conquests, as well as the allure of exoticism and intellectual exchange in their relationship.

In contrast, Alexander's marriage to Darius III's daughter Stateira, or Barsine as she was otherwise known, was a purely political alliance, devoid of any romantic sentiment. The union was aimed at solidifying Alexander's grip on power and growing stability in his empire. Unlike his marriage to Roxana, which was marked by genuine affection and mutual attraction, Alexander's relationship with Stateira was defined by practicality rather than passion. Their marriage symbolized the merging of Macedonian and Persian royal families, serving as a strategic maneuver to diminish dissent and consolidate Alexander's authority (*Stateira/Barsine*, 1999).

While the specific influence of his relationships with Barsine and Stateira on Alexander's decisions and leadership may be difficult to pinpoint, it is reasonable to assume that they played a role in shaping his broader diplomatic and strategic objectives. The alliances formed through these relationships likely influenced Alexander's interactions with Persian elites and his efforts to integrate Persian culture into his empire. The presence of Parysatis and Stateira in Alexander's inner circle may have also provided him with valuable insights and perspectives on Persian society and customs, informing his governance of conquered territories (Greenwalt, n.d.).

Unraveling Alexander's Identity

Throughout this chapter, we've looked into the multifaceted character of Alexander the Great, exploring the personal relationships that shaped his reign. From his military genius and strategic innovations to his embrace of Persian customs and the dynamics of his relationships with companions and romantic interests, we've gained a deeper understanding of the man behind the myth. Alexander's conquests were not just about territorial expansion; they may suggest a vision of cultural synthesis and unity, but (more importantly, they testify to his unsurpassed ability to inspire loyalty and devotion among his followers.

As we reflect on the aspects of Alexander's leadership and the personal dynamics that influenced his rule, it becomes evident that his legacy goes beyond conquests. His impact on the world was profound, reshaping the course of history and leaving a lasting mark on the cultures and peoples he encountered. Yet, with his untimely death, a void was left in the wake of his ambitions, sparking debates and mythologizing his legacy.

Moving forward, the next chapter will unravel the enduring legacy of a conqueror whose ambitions reshaped the world. We'll explore the lasting impact of his conquests, the complexities of succession and governance in the aftermath of his death, and how his legacy continues to be interpreted and debated by historians and scholars.

Chapter 8: The Legacy of a Conqueror

In the wake of Alexander the Great's untimely death, his legend was cemented in eternity. The man who sought to conquer the world left behind a legacy that would shape the course of history. But what is the truth behind his mysterious demise, and how did his dreams of empire influence the world long after he was gone?

In this chapter, we explore the mysterious circumstances surrounding Alexander's death and the immediate aftermath. We'll examine the complexity of his conquests, the lasting impact they had on the ancient world, and the far-reaching implications they held for future generations.

The Final Days and the Mystery of Alexander's Death

In the final days of his remarkable journey, Alexander the Great found himself in the clutches of the cruel hand of fate, his once unyielding spirit now touched by the fragility of mortality.

The Onset of Illness

During a series of grand feasts at Babylon in 323 B.C.E., at the age of 32, Alexander suddenly fell ill. He suffered a sudden collapse and endured intense pain. For 10 days, he battled a high fever that left him unable to speak, stripping him of his usual authority. During those days, there were fleeting moments of lucidity. It is said that in his final hours, Alexander was able to acknowledge those at his bedside with his eyes, a silent communion with the soldiers who had marched alongside him. In his eyes lay the weight of an empire, the echoes of conquests past, and the silent plea of a man who had dared to defy the bounds of mortal ambition.

Theories and Speculations

The circumstances surrounding Alexander's death are shrouded in mystery, captivating the minds of scholars. Historical records offer fragmented glimpses into Alexander's final days, each account presenting its version of events. Some describe his sudden collapse during a banquet followed by a lengthy illness characterized by fever and agonizing pain. Others mention his gradual decline over several weeks, with symptoms ranging from weakness to paralysis. However, despite these accounts, a clear picture of Alexander's final moments remains elusive.

Among the many theories proposed, one of the most perplexing aspects is the condition of his body post-mortem. Reports suggest a curious phenomenon: his body showed no decomposition for six days – a puzzling occurrence that has fuled speculation for centuries.

The Dying Alexander bust in the National Art Museum of Azerbaijan (Meniashvili, 2013). Marble copy of a Greek bronze from the 2nd century BC.

Ancient and modern observers were baffled by this unusual preservation, sparking a debate that Alexander may have been alive, though in a paralyzed state, when he was pronounced dead. Dr. Katherine Hall's proposition of Guillain-Barré syndrome adds another layer to the mystery. This autoimmune disorder affects the peripheral nervous system, where the body's immune system mistakenly attacks its nerves, leading to inflammation and damage. This results in muscle weakness, numbness, and tingling sensations, which can progress rapidly and lead to paralysis in severe cases. Guillain-Barré syndrome could have rendered Alexander comatose with minimal signs of life, potentially leading to a premature declaration of death. This would mean that Alexander was alive when the embalming process began, resulting in his death due to disembowelment (Hall, 2018).

Despite these intriguing speculations, the true cause of Alexander's demise remains elusive. Theories have emerged over the years, ranging from infectious diseases like typhoid fever and malaria—all common afflictions in ancient Babylon—to the persistent suspicion of poisoning. Historical accounts detailing symptoms such as chills, sweats, exhaustion, high fever, and severe abdominal pain align with those of typhoid fever, giving additional weight to this theory. Suspicions of foul play cast a shadow over various individuals, extending from Alexander's wives and generals to his illegitimate half-brother (Schep et al., 2013).

Alexander's Impact on History and Cultures

Alexander's death triggered a period of instability and upheaval that reshaped the balance of power in his vast empire.

The Immediate Aftermath of Alexander's Death

With no clear heir designated by Alexander, his death plunged the empire into a succession crisis. Within days, factions began fighting for control, leading to political intrigue, power struggles, and military conflicts. Alexander's generals, known as the *Diadochoi*, competed for dominance and sought to carve out their spheres of influence.

While the Diadochi were occupied with their power struggles, the remainder of Alexander's empire found itself experiencing widespread rebellions. In Greece, there was a revolt against Macedonian rule when many Greek city-states saw an opportunity to assert their independence in the power vacuum left by Alexander's death. In the Lamian War (323-322 B.C.E.), several city-states, including Athens, rose against Macedonian garrisons and attempted to throw off their control.

In the eastern provinces of the empire, there were numerous rebellions, some by settled Greek mercenaries, others by local populations, and still others by local governors seeking to assert their autonomy or independence. They saw the chaos following Alexander's death as the only chance to challenge Macedonian control. For many of them, they were right, and many of the furthest eastern provinces became independent kingdoms.

In Egypt, which had been conquered by Alexander in 332 B.C.E., there was a rebellion against Macedonian rule led by the native Egyptian population. The revolt was sparked by discontent with Macedonian taxation and administration. The Egyptian satrap, Cleomenes, attempted to assert independence from Macedonian control but was eventually defeated by Macedonian forces loyal to Alexander's successors.

In the aftermath of Alexander's death, his empire was divided among his generals, who established separate kingdoms known as the Hellenistic successor states. These included the Ptolemaic Kingdom in Egypt, the Seleucid Empire in Asia, the Antigonid Kingdom in Macedonia, and smaller states ruled by lesser Diadochi. This division marked the beginning of the Hellenistic period, characterized by the increased spread of Greek culture and influence throughout the Near East and beyond.

The most significant rebellions occurred among the Diadochi, who vied for control of the empire in the power vacuum left by Alexander's death. These power struggles led to a series of conflicts known as the Wars of the Diadochi, as rival generals fought for supremacy and sought to carve out their territories from the fragments of Alexander's empire (Bileta, 2022b).

The Long-Term Impact of Alexander's Conquests

Alexander had a far-reaching impact on the ancient world, shaping the course of history and leaving an enduring legacy that echoed across continents and centuries. Beyond the immediate political upheaval and military conquests, Alexander's campaigns fostered cultural exchange, facilitated the spread of Greek language and ideas, and laid the groundwork for the emergence of the Hellenistic Era.

The process of Hellenization, triggered by Alexander's conquests, stands as one of the most enduring legacies of his empire. Hellenization refers to the spread of Greek language, culture, and population into the vast territories of the former Persian Empire and beyond, fundamentally transforming the political, social, and cultural landscape of the ancient world.

Central to the process of Hellenization were the cities founded by Alexander throughout his conquests. Approximately 20 cities bore his name, with Alexandria in Egypt being the most renowned. These cities were strategically located in key regions of the empire, serving as administrative and military hubs and facilitating the control and governance of newly conquered territories. They were often established on or near existing settlements, and they blended Greek urban planning with local architectural traditions.

The founding of these cities was accompanied by the settlement of Greek colonists, soldiers, and administrators who brought Greek language, customs, and institutions with them. These settlers formed the foundation of the new urban communities, serving as the driving force for cultural exchange and assimilation. Over time, these cities became melting pots where Greek and local cultures intermingled to give rise to a rich and eclectic blend of traditions.

Alexander's conquests opened up new trade routes and facilitated the exchange of goods, ideas, and cultures between East and West. The integration of regions from Greece and Egypt to Persia and India created a vast network of commercial connections that spanned continents. Trade routes like the Silk Road became arteries of commerce, linking distant lands and facilitating the exchange of commodities such as silk, spices, precious metals, and luxury goods.

The cultural impact of Hellenization extended beyond urban centers to include art, architecture, literature, and philosophy. Greek artistic styles and techniques spread throughout the empire, influencing local artistic traditions and producing distinctive syntheses of Greek and indigenous artistic forms. The construction of monumental buildings, temples, and theaters in the Greek architectural style left a lasting imprint on the urban landscape of the Hellenistic world.

Language played a crucial role in the process of Hellenization, with Greek becoming the dominant language of administration, commerce, and culture in many regions of the former Persian Empire. The spread of the Greek language facilitated communication and cultural exchange across diverse peoples and territories, creating a common linguistic bond (Bileta, 2022a).

The Legacy Lives On

In this chapter, we explored the legacy of Alexander the Great, focusing on the circumstances surrounding his mysterious death and the enduring impact of his conquests on the ancient world. We examined the theories surrounding Alexander's demise, from poisoning to infectious disease, highlighting the enduring mystery and intrigue that continues to surround his death.

We also discussed the profound influence of Alexander's conquests on culture, language, trade, and the spread of Hellenistic influences across the known world. His vision of a united world under one ruler inspired generations long after his passing, shaping the course of history and leaving an indelible mark on Western civilization.

As we transition to the next chapter, we will explore the turbulent period following Alexander's death when his closest companions and formidable generals vied for control of his vast empire. This period of succession crises and battles for control among his generals set the stage for the emergence of the Hellenistic Era, a pivotal time in the ancient world characterized by cultural exchange, political upheaval, and the enduring legacy of Alexander's conquests.

Chapter 9: The Succession Crisis

The death of a titan is never a simple affair, and in the case of Alexander, it sparked a succession crisis of unparalleled magnitude. No clear heir stood to inherit the vast landmass he had conquered, leaving a power vacuum that beckoned the ambitious and opportunistic to stake their claim upon the shattered remains of his empire.

So began an era of intrigue, betrayal, and ceaseless conflict, as the Diadochi, once united under the banner of their formidable leader, now clashed in a struggle for dominion. From the plains of Mesopotamia to the shores of the Mediterranean, the clash of arms echoed, as each general sought to carve out their realm from Alexander's sprawling legacy.

The Division of the Empire Among the Diadochi

Upon Alexander's death in 323 B.C.E., his empire, stretching from Macedon and Greece to India, fell into the hands of his trusted generals. Initially, they tried to govern the vast territories collectively, but their unity quickly crumbled under the weight of their ambitions. At the center of the power struggle were three key figures and their descendants: Antigonus I Monophthalmus, Seleucus I Nicator, and Ptolemy I Soter (Wasson, 2016b).

The Three Generals

Antigonus, also known as Antigonus the One-Eyed from the loss of one eye in battle, was one of Alexander's most experienced and capable generals. Born in Macedonia, he rose through the ranks alongside Alexander, earning a reputation for his military expertise and strategic insight. After Alexander's death, Antigonus emerged as one of the most ambitious Diadochi, seeking to establish himself as the ruler of an expansive territory encompassing Asia Minor, Syria, and parts of Persia. He claimed the throne of Macedon and established the Antigonid dynasty (306-168 B.C.E.), but the kingship of Alexander's homeland was disputed until after Antigonus' death in 301 (Volkmann, 1998). The dynasty lasted until the Battle of Pydna in 168, after which Macedon became part of the expanding Roman Republic.

Seleucus, a Macedonian nobleman, served as one of Alexander's most trusted generals during his conquests in Asia. Following Alexander's death, Seleucus seized the opportunity to carve out his kingdom in the eastern provinces of the empire. Known for his diplomatic skills and administrative abilities, Seleucus founded the Seleucid Empire (312-63 B.C.E.), which stretched from Asia Minor to the borders of India. His reign marked a period of cultural and economic prosperity in the Near East, although it was often marred by conflicts with rival successors and neighboring powers (Gill, 2018). The influence and territory of the Seleucids slowly diminished until it occupied only part of Syria. In 63, the Roman Pompey the Great waved away the rump state and organized Syria as a Roman province.

Ptolemy, an accomplished general and scholar, was a childhood friend and close companion of Alexander. After his death, Ptolemy seized control of Egypt, establishing the Ptolemaic Dynasty (305-30 B.C.E.) that would endure for nearly three centuries. Ptolemy was not only a skilled general but also a patron of the arts and scholarship, founding the famed Library of Alexandria (Lendering, 2004). The Ptolemies withstood the advancing Roman expansion by allying with the growing republic for over a century. They fared better than the other successor states, but the last real Ptolemaic monarch, the famous Cleopatra VII, chose the wrong side in the Roman Civil War between Octavian and Mark Antony. Antony and Cleopatra committed suicide in 30, permanently ending the last major Hellenistic kingdom in the West and ancient title of Pharaoh. Octavian, now Augustus, made Egypt a province of the Roman Empire in 27 B.C.E.

The Wars of the Diadochi

The time after Alexander's death is filled with complicated webs of alliances betrayals, and battles. Entire books are dedicated to the military and political history of the Hellenistic Period, and a full account lies beyond the scope of the current work.

Nevertheless, a quick chronological account can impress upon the reader the shifting tides of conflict.

Ptolemy I as Pharaoh of Egypt (Stella, 2019).

On his deathbed at Babylon in 323, Alexander bestowed his signet ring to his companion Perdiccas. Since Alexander's son by Roxana, the eventual Alexander IV, was not yet born when Alexander died, he had not formally designated an heir, and his elder half-brother Philip Arrhidaeus was considered by most to be mentally unfit to rule. After Alexander IV's birth, Perdiccas became regent. Unfortunately, Meleager, an infantry commander, supported Philip Arrhidaeus. After a brief conflict, Perdiccas determined that Arrhidaeus and Alexander could rule jointly, though he himself would be regent for the infant. The provinces were divvied up among all the generals. For the next couple of years, Perdiccas ruled at Babylon as tensions rose.

First War of the Diadochi (321–319 B.C.E.)

The First War of the Diadochi, spanning from 321 to 319 B.C.E., marked the beginning of the drawn-out struggle for dominance among the Diadochi. The conflict was ignited by simmering tensions and disputes over the regency, the distribution of satrapies, and the overarching question of who would assume leadership in the wake of Alexander's passing. With each general harboring ambitions and agendas, the fragile unity that had once bound them together beneath Alexander's banner swiftly disintegrated into open conflict.

Several of Alexander the Great's former generals contested control of the empire. The main conflict of this first round of hostilities was between Perdiccas and his rivals Ptolemy, Antigonus, Craterus, Antipater, and his son Cassander. Ultimately, Perdiccas led a failed invasion to dislodge Ptolemy from Egypt, during which he was assassinated by his own troops. Of the other main combatants, Craterus was killed at the Battle of the Hellespont in 321 against Eumenes, a minor Diadoch who was loyal to Perdiccas.

The First War of the Diadochi reached its peak in the Partition of Triparadisus in 321 B.C.E. This was a crucial event that sought to address the issues fueling discord among the generals. The Partition was orchestrated by the hugely respected Antipater (his prominence dated back to Philip's early days). Its main aim was to reorganize the vast territories of Alexander's empire among the competing factions. Of course, he named himself supreme regent and assigned himself Macedonia, Greece, and some other territories. However, rather than calming the unrest, the Partition served as a temporary pause in the ongoing power struggle.

The death of Antipater in 319 B.C.E. marked a major turning point in the conflict. He designated another of Philip's old officers, Polyperchon, as his heir over his own son Cassander. With the death of one of the leading figures of the old guard, power dynamics shifted once again. This paved the way for further instability and upheaval in the years to come (Wasson, 2016b).

Second War of the Diadochi (318—316 B.C.E.)

The Second War of the Diadochi, occurring between 318 and 316 B.C.E., marked another turbulent chapter in the struggle for supremacy among Alexander's successors. This conflict was fueled by ongoing disputes over control of the empire and the ambitions of the key figures Antigonus, Cassander, and Polyperchon.

Antigonus I Monophthalmus, one of the most formidable and ambitious of the Diadochi, emerged as a central figure in the Second War. With his military expertise and cunning strategy, Antigonus sought to expand his influence and assert his dominance over the empire, challenging the authority of his rivals.

The Second War of the Diadochi saw a complex web of alliances and betrayals as factions vied for advantage. Cassander, ruling over Macedon and Greece, aligned himself with Antigonus against Polyperchon, the regent appointed by his father Antipater. However, shifting loyalties added to the chaos of the conflict.

The pivotal Battle of Gabiene proved decisive in shaping the outcome of the Second War. Antigonus, leading a coalition of Diadochi forces, clashed with Eumenes, a loyalist to the late Perdiccas, and his allies. Despite Eumenes's tactical brilliance, Antigonus emerged victorious, solidifying his position as a dominant force in the empire.

The Second War further deepened the divisions within the empire, as rival factions fought for control over the fragmented territories of Alexander's conquests. While Antigonus strengthened his grip over Asia Minor and parts of the Near East, Cassander pressed his claim in Macedon and Greece. Arrhidaeus was killed, and Cassander had Olympias murdered, took control of Alexander IV and Roxana, and consolidate his control over Greece and Macedon (Wasson, 2016b). Polyperchon was much diminished and fled to southern Greece. In addition, Lysimachus maintained his control over Thrace, and Ptolemy was largely secure in Egypt.

Third War of the Diadochi (315–311 B.C.E.)

The Third War of the Diadochi spanned from 315 to 311 B.C.E. Led by Antigonus, this conflict was marked by his ambitious attempts to establish supremacy over Asia, facing opposition from the other Diadochi.

Antigonus, emboldened by his victories in the Second War of the Diadochi and seeking to expand his influence even further, launched a campaign to consolidate control over the vast territories of Asia. With his military might and strategic insight, Antigonus aimed to assert his dominance over the fragmented remnants of Alexander's empire.

Antigonus forged alliances with his son Demetrios and Polyperchon, while facing opposition from Cassander, Ptolemy, Seleucus, and Lysimachus, who sought to check his ambitions and preserve their spheres of influence. Unfortunately, though the war was hotly contested, Antigonus could not maintain control of significant parts of Asia, especially after Demetrios lost the Battle of Gaza to Ptolemy and Seleucus.

The Third War of the Diadochi concluded with a temporary peace agreement in 311 B.C.E., known as the Peace of the Dynasts. This treaty, brokered by Seleucus and Lysimachus, aimed to halt the hostilities and stabilize the region. Cassander maintained control of Macedon, Thessaly, and parts of Greece, while Lysimachus kept Thrace. Antigonus still maintained his base in Asia Minor, Syria, and Phoenicia while Seleucus controlled the east. Ptolemy continued to strengthen his control over Egypt and Cyprus. However, the peace proved fragile and did little to resolve the underlying tensions and rivalries among the Diadochi (Wasson, 2016b).

Babylonian War (311–309 B.C.E.)

The Babylonian War (311-309 B.C.E.), was primarily between Antigonus I Monophthalmus and Seleucus I Nicator. Following the conclusion of the Third War of the Diadochi, Antigonus emerged as one of the most powerful and ambitious of Alexander's successors. Seeking to assert his dominance over the eastern provinces of the empire, Antigonus launched a campaign to expand his territory into the heartland of Mesopotamia. However, Seleucus' supporters were able to repel Antigonus' forces, and the latter eventually had to concede that the eastern part of Alexander's empire now belonged to Seleucus.

The Babylonian War had far-reaching consequences for the balance of power among the Diadochi and the future of Alexander's empire. Seleucus' victory effectively ended any chance of reuniting the empire under a single ruler, as he established the Seleucid Empire in the eastern territories. This marked the beginning of a new era of Hellenistic kingdoms, with Seleucus laying the foundation for a powerful and enduring dynasty in the Near East (Lendering, 2002).

Fourth War of the Diadochi (307–301 B.C.E.)

Antigonus' ambitions flared up again in 307. The Fourth War of the Diadochi stands as the final major conflict among Alexander's successors, marking a decisive turning point in the struggle for supremacy and the reconfiguration of the empire.

Seleucus' attention was focused on the eastern extremities of his empire for several years, leaving several of his allies temporarily without his support. Antigonus and his son Demetrios again fought with Cassander, Ptolemy, and Lysimachus.

In 307, Demetrios took Athens and most of Greece, continuing on to defeat a Ptolemaic fleet off the coast of Cyprus. Antigonus attempted to invade Egypt, but inclement weather led to supply problems. Meanwhile, in 305, Demetrios besieged Rhodes. Ptolemy came to the city's aid, earning the moniker *Soter*, "savior." The following year, Demetrios moved to pacify Greece, where Cassander had retaken Athens. He did so successfully, but could not solidify his hold, since he had to lead his army to Asia Minor to aid his father against Lysimachus

The Fourth War culminated in the Battle of Ipsus, with both sides marshaling their forces and preparing for a decisive confrontation. Antigonus, bolstered by his son Demetrios' troops, sought to confront the coalition in a bid to secure victory and dominance. Antigonus and Demetrius commanded a formidable army, comprising Macedonian Phalanxes, cavalry, and light infantry. Seleucus had returned from the east and brought with him 500 Indian elephants to aid the coalition.

Demetrios led a strong cavalry charge that drove off the enemy horsemen, but he chased them too far and became separated from the battlefield. Seizing the moment, Seleucus blocked Demetrios' return with several hundred of his war elephants, trapping him away from the fight.

With no cavalry to protect its flank, Antigonus's infantry phalanx was left exposed. Seleucus and his allies surrounded the soldiers and attacked from all sides. Some of Antigonus' troops fled or even switched sides. Antigonus, now alone in the center, was killed along with many of his men by enemy javelins. His army collapsed, and the battle was lost. The dream of putting Alexander's empire back together died with him.

Following the defeat of Antigonus at Ipsus, the surviving Diadochi formalized the division of Alexander's empire into separate realms. Seleucus, Lysimachus, Cassander, and Ptolemy each carved out their territories, laying the foundation for the Hellenistic kingdoms that would dominate the ancient world in the centuries to come (Wasson, 2016b).

Alexander's Death and the Stability of His Empire

Alexander's charismatic leadership provided a unifying vision for his conquests, inspiring his soldiers with a sense of purpose and destiny. However, with his death, this unifying force disappeared, leaving the empire without a clear direction or sense of purpose. Without a strong central authority to hold the empire together, the disparate regions began to assert their autonomy, further contributing to its disintegration.

Another factor that escalated the disintegration of the empire was its cultural and ethnic diversity. Alexander's conquests had brought together peoples from diverse backgrounds and cultures, creating a complex mosaic of identities within the empire. The absence of a unifying leader or ideology to bridge these differences made it difficult to maintain cohesion, leading to tensions and conflicts among the various ethnic and cultural groups (Sherry, n.d.).

The Forces that Fractured the Empire

The ambitions of the Diadochi were often driven by regional loyalties and interests. As they sought to expand their influence, they clashed over control of specific territories and strategic assets. These regional rivalries further divided the empire along geographic lines, undermining any attempts at centralized governance and fostering a climate of instability and conflict. Without a unified vision or central authority to guide their actions, the generals pursued their agendas independently, leading to disjointed and inconsistent governance. This lack of coordination weakened the empirc's ability to respond to external threats and internal challenges.

The intense competition among the Diadochi also fostered an atmosphere of distrust and betrayal. Loyalties were constantly shifting as alliances were formed and broken in pursuit of power. This atmosphere of intrigue and uncertainty made it difficult to build trust and cooperation among the generals, hindering efforts to govern the empire effectively.

The empire included Greek, Persian, Egyptian, Indian, and numerous other ethnic groups, each with its customs, beliefs, and social structures. Governing such a diverse population required sensitivity to cultural differences and the implementation of policies that respected and accommodated these varied identities. While Greek was the *lingua franca* of the ruling elite, it was not universally spoken throughout the empire. Communication between regions and administrative centers was often hindered by language barriers, making it difficult to disseminate orders, enforce laws, and maintain cohesion across the empire.

Some regions within the empire resisted centralized rule, preferring local autonomy and self-governance. These areas often rebelled against attempts to impose foreign rule or cultural hegemony, leading to protracted conflicts and instability. The Diadochi conflicts deepened these tensions as rival generals vied for control over different regions, further destabilizing the empire (Sherry, n.d.).

The Great Fragmentation

The succession crisis following Alexander the Great's death plunged his empire into a spiral of intrigue, betrayal, and incessant warfare, fundamentally altering the political landscape of the ancient world. The ambitions of the Diadochi, once united under Alexander's banner, turned against each other in a ruthless struggle for power, leading to the division of the empire into warring Hellenistic kingdoms.

Despite Alexander's dream of a unified empire under his rule, the lack of a clear successor and the clashing ambitions of his generals shattered that vision. However, while his empire fractured, the legacy of Alexander endured. His conquests spread Greek culture, language, and ideas throughout the known world, leaving an indelible mark on history.

The Hellenistic World after the death of Seleucus I Nicator
(Avantiputra7, 2024).

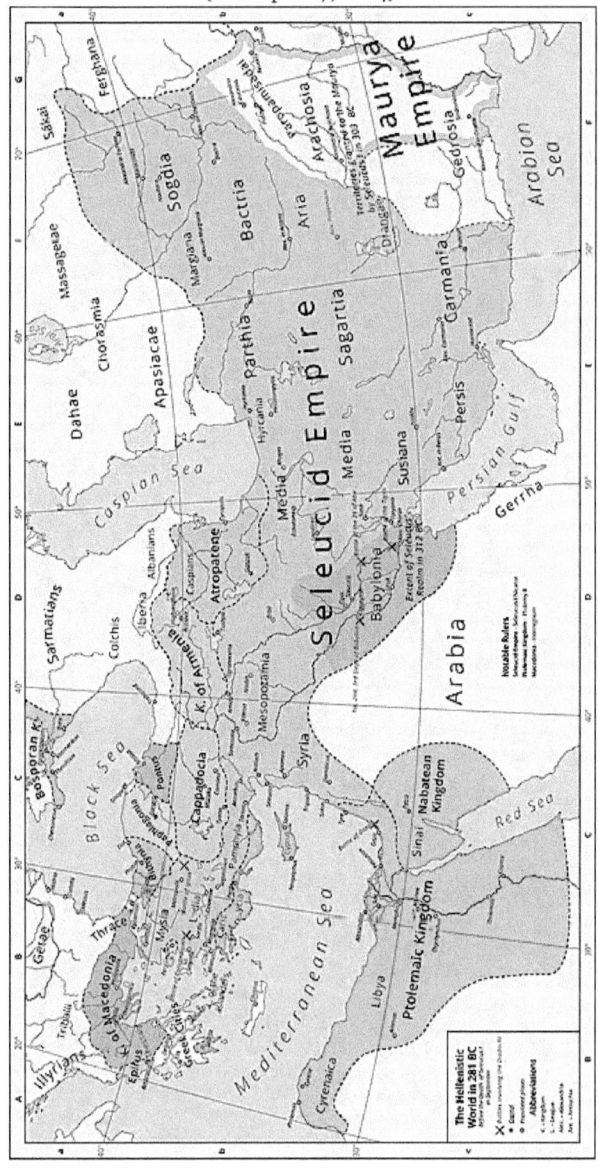

Chapter 10: Alexander Through the Ages

More than two millennia after his death, Alexander the Great continues to live on in history books, movies, literature, and the collective imagination of cultures around the world. Why does his story continue to fascinate us?

In this chapter, we look at the complexities of Alexander's historical portrayal and the diverse perspectives on his character and ambitions. From conqueror to visionary, from hero to tyrant, Alexander's image has been subject to interpretation and reevaluation across centuries and continents.

Alexander's Portrayal in History and Media

From ancient chronicles to the silver screen, the narrative surrounding Alexander has undergone a remarkable evolution, reflecting the diverse interpretations and cultural perspectives that have shaped his image over time. By comparing historical accounts with cinematic depictions, we unravel the complexities of Alexander's character, ambitions, and legacy. Through this exploration, we aim to identify the intersections between historical truth and mythological embellishment, shedding light on the fascination that surrounds one of history's most enigmatic figures.

Alexander in Historical Texts

The portrayal of Alexander the Great in historical texts has undergone a significant evolution from ancient times to today, reflecting the shifting perspectives and cultural contexts of different eras. In ancient accounts such as those by Arrian, Plutarch, and Quintus Curtius Rufus, Alexander was often depicted as a heroic conqueror, a brilliant military strategist, and a symbol of Hellenistic civilization's triumph over the Persian Empire. These narratives emphasized Alexander's military prowess, his legendary exploits, and his ambitious quest to create a vast empire stretching from Greece to India (Mark, 2013).

The *Alexander Romance* illustrates the almost superhuman imprint of Alexander on cultures across the globe. The original version may have been a Greek text of the late 3rd century C.E.; however, it quickly spread into different cultures and each reception gave birth to many new legends that accrued over a thousand years. Different versions of the *Romance* under many different titles exist in dozens of languages – all the European and Middle-Eastern ones, of course, but even Mongolian and Malaysian. In them, Alexander appeared as a cultural hero in nearly every area of the world, from the man who built a wall to repel the apocalyptic Gog and

Magog in early Christian and Muslim stories, to an exemplar of knightly virtue in 12th century Europe (The Editors of Encyclopaedia Britannica, 1998).

As time progressed, Alexander's image became more nuanced and subject to reinterpretation. During the Renaissance period, scholars like Leonardo Bruni and Niccolò Machiavelli viewed Alexander as a model ruler and strategist, drawing parallels between his conquests and the expansionist ambitions of contemporary European monarchs. On the other hand, Enlightenment thinkers such as Voltaire and Rousseau critiqued Alexander's imperialistic tendencies and authoritarian rule. They focused on the moral complexities of his reign (Daniotti, 2022).

Portrait of Niccolò Machiavelli by Santi di Tito (ca. 1550-1560) (Gun, 2010).

In the modern era, Alexander's portrayal has continued to evolve in response to changing political, social, and cultural dynamics. While some historians, like Ernst Badian and Robin Lane Fox, have sought to rehabilitate Alexander's image as a visionary leader and cultural unifier, others have scrutinized his actions through a more critical lens, examining the human cost of his conquests and the impact of his legacy on the peoples he subjugated (Thomas, 1968).

The changing depictions of Alexander in historical texts mirror the relationship between interpretations of history, cultural norms, and ideological motives. As societal views on empire, conquest, and governance evolve, so too does our perception and evaluation of the great figures of the past. Despite claims of objectivity (sometimes sincere, sometimes not), the nature of historical understanding is dynamic.

Alexander in Film, Literature, and Art

Alexander's representation in various media forms has played a crucial role in perpetuating his myth and contributing to the larger-than-life image surrounding him. In film, notable productions like *Alexander* by Oliver Stone and *Alexander the Great* by Robert Rossen depict him as a charismatic leader. They often emphasize his military conquests and romanticize his adventures across vast territories. These cinematic portrayals often amplify the grandeur of his exploits, portraying him as a larger-than-life figure destined for greatness (Ebert, 2004).

Literature has also been instrumental in mythologizing Alexander's persona for modern consumption. Writers like Mary Renault, in her acclaimed novels *Fire from Heaven* and *The Persian Boy*, have explored the psychological complexities of Alexander's character. She portrays him as a flawed yet charismatic figure, driven by ambition and inner demons. These literary works add a modern veneer to Alexander's legend. They explore his relationships, motivations, and inner conflicts to contribute to his myth as a complex and enigmatic quasi-historical figure (Renault, 1969 and 1972).

In art, Alexander has been depicted in various media, from ancient sculptures and mosaics to Renaissance paintings and contemporary artwork. These artistic representations often idealize Alexander, portraying him as a heroic conqueror or a divine ruler, embodying the values and aspirations of the cultures that produced them. Through iconic images like the Alexander Mosaic or depictions of his legendary encounter with the Gordian Knot, artists have perpetuated his myth as a symbol of power, ambition, and conquest (Hemingway & Hemingway, 2004).

Collectively, these representations contribute to the mythologizing of Alexander by presenting him as a larger-than-life figure whose exploits transcend the boundaries of history. They glorify his military conquests, personal charisma, and cultural impact, thereby cementing Alexander's legacy as one of the most enduring figures in human history. Moreover, they ensure that his legend will continue to captivate and inspire audiences across generations.

The Debate Over Alexander's Character and Ambitions

Alexander the Great is a towering figure whose legacy evokes both admiration and controversy. As we examine the depths of his character and actions, a compelling debate emerges: Was Alexander the Great a ruthless conqueror driven by insatiable ambition, or was he a visionary leader whose conquests paved the way for cultural exchange and enlightenment? This question invites us to explore the complexities of Alexander's persona and the lasting impact of his reign on the course of human civilization.

Alexander the Ruthless Conqueror?

The view of Alexander as nothing more than a ruthless conqueror is based on analyzing the historical records portraying his deeds and their aftermath. Critics highlight instances of brutality in Alexander's campaigns, such as the merciless suppression of revolts and the execution of perceived traitors, as evidence of his single-minded pursuit of power. The heavy toll exacted on both his soldiers and the populations of conquered territories is cited as further proof of his disregard for human life and welfare in the pursuit of his ambitions.

Critics point to the dissolution of Alexander's empire shortly after his death as an indication of the lack of foresight and wisdom in his governance. His failure to establish a clear and sustainable succession plan is interpreted as evidence of a leadership style driven more by personal glory and ambition than by a coherent long-term strategy for governance. Critics argue that Alexander's conquests were fueled by a reckless pursuit of fame and immortality, characterized by a "crazy dream of glory" rather than a genuine concern for the well-being of the lands and peoples he conquered.

In this interpretation, Alexander is a figure whose legacy is tarnished by the human cost of his conquests and the instability that followed in their wake. From this perspective, his achievements are overshadowed by the suffering and destruction brought about by his relentless pursuit of power, leading some to view him as a tyrant and glorified butcher rather than an enlightened monarch (Mark, 2013).

Alexander the Visionary Leader?

By others, Alexander is celebrated as a transformative figure whose actions reshaped the course of history. Advocates of this view emphasize Alexander's role as a champion of Greek culture and highlight the profound impact of his conquests on the spread of Greek language, philosophy, and art across diverse regions of the ancient world.

Central to this interpretation is Alexander's establishment of cities that served as strongholds of Greek culture and centers of learning, facilitating cultural exchange and intellectual development. These cities, such as Alexandria in Egypt and Alexandria Eschate in modern Tajikistan became hubs of trade and cultural diffusion.

Supporters of this viewpoint see his military campaigns as evidence of strategic brilliance and innovative tactics. His ability to inspire unwavering loyalty in his troops, even in the face of daunting challenges and grueling campaigns, is regarded as a testament to his charismatic leadership qualities.

Advocates argue that Alexander's impact transcends mere conquest. He is revered as a forward-looking leader whose aspiration for a unified empire fostered centuries of cultural exchange and intellectual advancement (Bullari, 2020).

Alexander's Enduring Fascination

Alexander's lasting appeal can be attributed to a multitude of factors, each stemming from the remarkable events that punctuated his life. His unparalleled military achievements, beginning with the conquest of the mighty Persian Empire, captured the imagination of generations, cementing his reputation as one of history's greatest military commanders. His daring vision, epitomized by the creation of a vast empire stretching from Greece to India, inspired awe and admiration as it showcased his boundless ambition and determination to leave a lasting mark on the world.

The founding of Alexandria is a testament to Alexander's legacy as a visionary leader, as he sought to establish cities that served as beacons of knowledge and culture. His efforts to spread Greek culture manifested through the promotion of Greek language, art, and philosophy, contributed to the cultural enrichment of the lands he conquered. It left a permanent imprint on the course of history. Additionally, Alexander's military innovations, like the use of combined arms and strategic maneuvering, revolutionized warfare and continue to influence military strategy to this day.

The dramatic events of Alexander's life, from his legendary crossing of the Hellespont to the epic Siege of Tyre and the exploration of the mysterious Indus Valley, captivated the imagination of contemporaries and continue to inspire fascination in modern times. His promotion of religious pluralism, exemplified by his respectful treatment of (and participation in) the religions of the conquered set a precedent for enlightened governance and tolerance in a world often torn apart by religious strife.

The Importance of Alexander's Story in Modern Culture

Alexander's story holds a respected place in modern culture, serving as a timeless source of inspiration. His remarkable life, characterized by unparalleled conquests, visionary ambitions, and dramatic narrative arcs, continues to captivate the imagination of people around the world.

One of the key reasons for Alexander's enduring appeal is the universal themes embedded within his story. His journey from a young prince to a world-conquering emperor resonates with audiences as a classic tale of ambition, adventure, and triumph. The complexities of his character, including his charisma, intelligence, and flaws, make him a compelling and relatable figure, despite the millennia separating modern audiences from his era (Kets De Vries, 2014).

As long as storytellers and audiences are seeking a source of motivation, Alexander's story will continue to inspire, ensuring that his legend lives on in modern culture.

Legends Never Die

As we close this chapter of *Alexander Unleashed* we are reminded of the complexity and enduring nature of his legacy. From the battlefields of Asia to the silver screen, Alexander the Great has become a symbol of ambition, conquest, and the eternal quest for greatness. As we reflect on his life and the vast

empire he built, we come to understand that
Alexander's true conquest has been his lasting impact
on history, culture, and the hearts of those who
continue to be inspired by his legendary story.

Sardonyx cameo of Alexander the Great. Possibly by Pyrgoteles, Alexander's
personal engraver (World Imaging, 2006) ca. 325 BC.

Conclusion

In this book, we aimed to unravel the enigma of Alexander, to peel back the layers of myth and legend that have shrouded his story for millennia. Through the tumultuous landscape of ancient history, one truth emerges with striking clarity: Alexander was driven by an unquenchable thirst for greatness, a hunger that could only be sated by the conquest of the known world.

We've come to understand that greatness is not merely the accumulation of power or wealth, but the realization of one's fullest potential. In Alexander's relentless pursuit of conquest, we find echoes of our aspirations and our desires to leave a mark upon the world. His journey serves as a beacon of inspiration, illuminating the path for those who dare to dream boldly and act courageously.

In the wake of his conquests, Alexander forged an empire that stretched from Greece to the edges of the known world, a testament to the boundless potential of human endeavor. But his true legacy does not lie in the territories he claimed or the battles he waged, but in the hearts and minds of those who came after him. His vision of unity and enlightenment, of a world bound together by the ties of common humanity, continues to inspire generations.

In the spirit of Alexander, let us embark upon our odyssey, charting a course through uncharted waters and scaling the heights of our ambitions. Let us seize the day with the same determination that drove Alexander to conquer the world, knowing that the greatest triumphs lie not in the destination, but in the journey itself. In the words of Alexander himself, "There is nothing impossible to him who will try."

Note to the Reader

Sharing sincere feedback is the best way to support (and improve) the work of independent publishers. If you enjoyed and found value in this book, please leave a review and invite others to learn about and reflect upon our common past to build a promising future.

Scan the code below to leave a review!

References

Alexander's Crossing of the Hindu Kush and his Campaigns in India. (2023, December 5). Pro-Papers. Retrieved February 13, 2025, from https://pro-papers.com/samples/history/alexander-the-great/alexander-s-crossing-of-the-hindu-kush-and-his-campaigns-in-india

Alexander the Great's sister: Cleopatra of Macedonia (354-308 BC). (2022, May 17). Totally History. Retrieved February 11, 2025, from https://totallyhistory.com/alexander-the-greats-sister-cleopatra/

Alexander the Great's vision for an empire: Governance and administration. (2023, December 4). Pro-Papers. Retrieved February 13, 2025, from https://pro-papers.com/samples/history/alexander-the-great/vision-for-an-empire--governance-and-administration

Amyntas IV of Macedon. (n.d.). Alexanderthegreat.org. Retrieved February 11, 2025, from https://alexander-the-great.org/people/amyntas-IV-of-macedon

Arrian. (1884). *The Anabasis of Alexander* [Online PDF]. In E. J. Chinnock (Trans.), Wikisource. Hodder and Stoughton. https://en.wikisource.org/wiki/The_Anabasis_of_Alexander

Arrian. (c. 327 B.C.). *Anabasis.* The Latin Library. Retrieved February 13, 2025, from https://www.thelatinlibrary.com/imperialism/readings/arrian.html

Bileta, V. (2022a). *What was the Hellenistic world like? Alexander the Great's legacy.* TheCollector. Retrieved February 13, 2025, from https://www.thecollector.com/hellenistic-world-alexander-the-great-legacy/

Bileta, V. (2022b). *Hellenistic Kingdoms: The worlds of Alexander the Great's heirs.* TheCollector. Retrieved February 13, 2025, from https://www.thecollector.com/major-hellenistic-kingdoms/

Biography.com Editors. (2021, June 29). Alexander the Great. *Biography.* https://www.biography.com/political-figures/alexander-the-great

Bullari, D. (2020, November 30). *The visionary leadership of Alexander the Great* (The Foreign Journal, Ed.). Medium. Retrieved February 22, 2025, from https://theforeignjournal.medium.com/the-visionary-leadership-of-alexander-the-great-e17cf327c867

Carey, C. (2021, September 21). The Persian Invasion of 480 BC: 2500 years on. *Cambridge Core Blog.* Retrieved February 6, 2025, from https://www.cambridge.org/core/blog/2021/09/21/the-persian-invasion-of-480-bc-2500-years-on/

Carney, E. (1992). The Politics of Polygamy: Olympias, Alexander and the Murder of Philip. Historia: *Zeitschrift Für Alte Geschichte, 41*(2), 169–189. http://www.jstor.org/stable/4436236

Cartwright, M. (2025). Peloponnesian war. *World History Encyclopedia.* https://www.worldhistory.org/timeline/Peloponnesian_War/

Choubineh, N. (2024). Thessalonike of Macedon. In *World History Encyclopedia.* Retrieved February 7, 2025, from https://www.worldhistory.org/Thessalonike_of_Macedon/

Daniotti, C. (2022). The emergence of a new Renaissance iconography in the fifteenth century. In *Reinventing Alexander: Myth, Legend, History in Renaissance Italian Art.* Brepolis. https://www.brepols.net/products/IS-9782503597430-1

De Santis, M. (2001, December). *The Battle of Gaugamela: Alexander the Great vs. Darius III.* Warfare History Network. Retrieved February 11, 2025, from https://warfarehistorynetwork.com/article/the-battle-of-gaugamela-alexander-the-great-vs-darius-iii

Ebert, R. (2004, November 23). *'Alexander' not so great movie review (2004).* RogerEbert.com. Retrieved February

22, 2025, from
https://www.rogerebert.com/reviews/alexander-2004
Ferguson, J. (1998). Hellenistic age. In *Encyclopaedia Britannica*. Retrieved February 22, 2025, from
https://www.britannica.com/event/Hellenistic-Age
Fisher, M. (n.d.). *Roxana: the Bactrian Queen of Alexander the Great*. martinifisher.com. Retrieved February 13, 2025, from
https://martinifisher.com/2025/01/14/roxana-the-bactrian-queen-of-alexander-the-great/
Garlinghouse, T. (2022, March 14). *The rise and fall of the Great Library of Alexandria*. livescience.com. Retrieved February 13, 2025, from
https://www.livescience.com/rise-and-fall-of-the-great-alexandria-library
Gill, N. (2018, September 7). *Seleucus, the successor of Alexander*. ThoughtCo. Retrieved February 21, 2025, from https://www.thoughtco.com/who-was-seleucus-116847
Goldsworthy, A. (2023, August 23). *Did Alexander the Great arrange his father's murder?* HISTORY. Retrieved February 11, 2025, from
https://www.history.com/news/alexander-the-great-father-philip-murder
Greenwalt, W. (n.d.). Parysatis II (c. 350–323 BCE). In *Encyclopedia.com*. Retrieved February 13, 2025, from
https://www.encyclopedia.com/women/encyclopedias-almanacs-transcripts-and-maps/parysatis-ii-c-350-323-bce
Griego, M. (2023, May 13). *Alexander the Great in DANIEL 8*. Biblical Viewpoint.
https://biblicalviewpoint.com/2023/05/12/alexander-the-great-in-daniel-8/
Griffith, G. (n.d.). *Philip II of Macedon (382-336 B.C.)*. The Latin Library. Retrieved February 6, 2025, from
https://www.thelatinlibrary.com/imperialism/notes/philip2.html
Hall, K. (2018). Did Alexander the Great Die from Guillaine-Barre Syndrome? [Journal-article]. *The Ancient History Bulletin, 32*(3 and 4), 106–128.

https://www.ancienthistorybulletin.org/subscribed-users-area/wp-content/uploads/2018/12/hall.pdf

Hammond, N. (1992). Alexander's Charge at the Battle of Issus in 333 B.C. *Historia: Zeitschrift Für Alte Geschichte,* *41*(4), 395–406. http://www.jstor.org/stable/4436258

Hays, J. (2024, September). *Alexander the Great's personal life: wives, friends, lovers, children.* Facts and Details. Retrieved February 7, 2025, from https://europe.factsanddetails.com/article/entry-931.html#chapter-0

Hemingway, S., & Hemingway, C. (2004, October). *The rise of Macedon and the conquests of Alexander the Great.* The Met's Heilbrunn Timeline of Art History. Retrieved February 6, 2025, from https://www.metmuseum.org/toah/hd/alex/hd_alex.htm

Hephaestion. (n.d.). Alexanderthegreat.org. Retrieved February 13, 2025, from https://alexander-the-great.org/people/hephaestion

Historia Civilis. (2017, July 5). *Macedonian battle tactics* [Video]. YouTube. Retrieved February 13, 2025, from https://www.youtube.com/watch?v=juH-ckrN-cQ

Holmes, R. (2022, January 19). *What Happened when Alexander the Great Visited the Oracle at Siwa?* TheCollector. Retrieved February 13, 2025, from https://www.thecollector.com/alexander-the-great-oracle-siwa/

Holmes, R. (2024, June 18). *Alexander's Destruction of Thebes in 335 BCE (Battle & Aftermath).* TheCollector. Retrieved February 11, 2025, from https://www.thecollector.com/alexander-the-great-destruction-thebes/

Hughes, T. (2023, July 13). City Stormers: *The formidable siege engines of Alexander the Great.* History Hit. Retrieved February 13, 2025, from https://www.historyhit.com/city-stormers-the-formidable-siege-engines-of-alexander-the-great/

Invicta. (2021, February 21). *Units of History - The Macedonian Companion Cavalry DOCUMENTARY* [Video]. YouTube. Retrieved February 13, 2025, from https://www.youtube.com/watch?v=bbLnrGGqyWY

Kets De Vries, M. (2014, November 18). *11 Leadership Lessons from Alexander the Great*. INSEAD Knowledge. Retrieved February 22, 2025, from https://knowledge.insead.edu/leadership-organisations/11-leadership-lessons-alexander-great

Kholod, M. M. (2024). The Administration of Alexander's Empire. In D. Ogden (Ed.), *The Cambridge Companion to Alexander the Great* (pp. 290–316). Cambridge University Press.

Kikoy, H. (2018, July 20). *The Grand Master: Alexander's Genius in the Battle of Issus*. War History Online. Retrieved February 11, 2025, from https://www.warhistoryonline.com/instant-articles/alexanders-genius-battle-issus.html

Kings and Generals. (2018, September 6). *Alexander the Great: Logistics* [Video]. YouTube. Retrieved February 13, 2025, from https://www.youtube.com/watch?v=ahfyIxLlbGA

Lau, J. (n.d.). *Third Sacred War (356–346 BC)*. Stories Preschool. Retrieved February 6, 2025, from https://www.storiespreschool.com/third_sacred_war.html

Lendering, J. (2002). *Diadochi 6: The Babylonian War*. Livius.org. Retrieved February 21, 2025, from https://www.livius.org/articles/concept/diadochi/diadochi-6-the-babylonian-war/

Lendering, J. (2004). *Ptolemy I Soter*. Livius.org. Retrieved February 21, 2025, from https://www.livius.org/articles/person/ptolemy-i-soter/

Liao, Z. (2024). How Alexanders Relationship with Olympias Impacted His Achievement and Ultimate Downfall. *Communications in Humanities Research, 29*(1), 209–213. https://doi.org/10.54254/2753-7064/29/20230739

Liebert, H. (2011). Alexander the Great and the history of globalization. *The Review of Politics, 73*(4), 533–560. https://doi.org/10.1017/s0034670511003639

Little, B. (2024, November 12). *Alexander the Great: 6 key battles and a Siege*. HISTORY. Retrieved February 11, 2025, from https://www.history.com/news/alexander-the-great-key-battles-empire

Mark, J. J. (2013). Alexander the Great. In *World History Encyclopedia*. Retrieved February 22, 2025, from https://www.worldhistory.org/Alexander_the_Great/

Monzani, G. P. (2025, January 5). *The influence of Alexander the Great on Indian and world cuisine*. Greek Reporter. Retrieved February 13, 2025, from https://greekreporter.com/2025/01/05/the-influence-of-alexander-the-great-on-indian-and-world-cuisine/

Olbrycht, M. J. (2014). "An Admirer of Persian Ways": Alexander the Great's reforms in Parthia-Hyrcania and the Iranian heritage [PDF]. In T. Daryaee, A. Mousavi, & K. Rezakhani (Eds.), *Excavating an Empire: Achaemenid Persia in longue duree* (pp. 37–62). Mazda Publishers. https://www.academia.edu/7370159/An_Admirer_of_Persian_Ways_Alexander_the_Greats_Reforms_in_Parthia_Hyrcania_and_the_Iranian_Heritage

Olympias. (n.d.). *In Oxford Reference*. Retrieved February 7, 2025, from https://www.oxfordreference.com/display/10.1093/oi/authority.20110803100249261

Philip Arrhidaeus. (2020, September 23). Livius.org. Retrieved February 11, 2025, from https://www.livius.org/articles/person/philip-arrhidaeus/

Pillai, G. (1937). Skanda: The Alexander Romance in India. In *Proceedings of the All-India Oriental Conference 1937* (pp. 955–976). https://murugan.org/research/Skanda.Alexander.Romance.in.India.pdf

Plutarch. (1919). *Plutarch's Lives* (B. Perrin, Trans.). Harvard University Press; William Heinemann Ltd. (Original work published ca. 100 C.E.)

Plutarch. (n.d.). *Plutarch on the battle on the Granicus* (Evelyn, Trans.). Livius.org. Retrieved February 11, 2025, from https://www.livius.org/sources/content/plutarch/plutarchs-alexander/battle-on-the-granicus/

Pollard, J., & Pollard, S. (2019). The Temple of Artemis burns. *History Today, 69*(7). Retrieved February 7, 2025, from https://www.historytoday.com/archive/months-past/temple-artemis-burns

Porus. (2002). Livius.org. Retrieved February 13, 2025, from https://www.livius.org/articles/person/porus

Proskynesis. (2019). Livius.org. Retrieved March 27, 2025, from https://www.livius.org/articles/concept/proskynesis/

Raikar, S.P. (n.d.). Battle of the Hydaspes. *Encyclopedia Britannica.* https://www.britannica.com/event/Battle-of-the-Hydaspes

Renault, M. (1969). *Fire from heaven.* Vintage.

Renault, M. (1972). *The Persian boy.* Vintage.

Rickard, J. (2016, November 17). *Social War 357-55 BC (Greece).* historyofwar.org. Retrieved February 6, 2025, from http://www.historyofwar.org/articles/wars_social_war_357-55.html

Rickard, J. (2016, December 16). *Siege of Amphipolis, 357 BC.* historyofwar.org. Retrieved February 6, 2025, from http://www.historyofwar.org/articles/siege_amphipolis_357.html#google_vignette

Rickard, J. (2017, January 27). *Peace of Philocrates, 346 BC.* historyofwar.org. Retrieved February 6, 2025, from https://www.historyofwar.org/articles/peace_philocrates.html

Roos, D. (2023, August 23). *How Alexander the Great conquered the Persian Empire.* HISTORY. Retrieved February 13, 2025, from https://www.history.com/news/alexander-the-great-defeat-persian-empire

Sanujit. (2011). *Cultural Links between India & the Greco-Roman World.* In World History Encyclopedia. Retrieved February 13, 2025, from https://www.worldhistory.org/article/208/cultural-links-between-india--the-greco-roman-worl/

Schep, L. J., Slaughter, R. J., Vale, J. A., & Wheatley, P. (2013). Was the death of Alexander the Great due to poisoning? Was it Veratrum album? *Clinical*

Toxicology, 52(1), 72–77.
https://doi.org/10.3109/15563650.2013.870341

Schools of Indian Philosophy. (n.d.). Drishti IAS. Retrieved February 13, 2025, from https://www.drishtiias.com/to-the-points/paper4/schools-of-indian-philosophy

Schumate, J. (2015, November 12). Philip II and the Macedonian Army. *War History.* Retrieved February 6, 2025, from https://warhistory.org/%40msw/article/philip-ii-and-the-macedonian-army

Sherry, B. (n.d.). *The Macedonian Empire.* Khan Academy. Retrieved February 21, 2025, from https://www.khanacademy.org/humanities/whp-origins/era-3-cities-societies-and-empires-6000-bce-to-700-c-e/36-the-growth-of-empires-betaa/a/read-the-macedonian-empire-beta

Stoogenke, L. (2024, March 4). *The political role of Hephaestion.* Classics for All. Retrieved February 13, 2025, from https://classicsforall.org.uk/reading-room/rostra/political-role-hephaestion

The Editors of Encyclopaedia Britannica. (n.d.). Battle of Gaugamela. In *Encyclopaedia Britannica.* Retrieved February 11, 2025, from https://www.britannica.com/event/Battle-of-Gaugamela

The Editors of Encyclopaedia Britannica. (n.d.). League of Corinth. In *Encyclopaedia Britannica.* Retrieved February 10, 2025, from https://www.britannica.com/topic/League-of-Corinth

The Editors of Encyclopaedia Britannica. (1998). Alexander romance. In Encyclopaedia Britannica. Retrieved March 24, 2025, from https://www.britannica.com/art/Alexander-romance

The Editors of Encyclopaedia Britannica. (1998). Lysimachus. In *Encyclopaedia Britannica.* Retrieved February 21, 2025, from https://www.britannica.com/biography/Lysimachus

The Editors of Encyclopaedia Britannica. (2024, December 19). Greco-Persian Wars. The Ionian Revolt. In *Encyclopaedia Britannica.*

https://www.britannica.com/event/Greco-Persian-Wars/The-Ionian-Revolt-499-493-bce

The Editors of Encyclopaedia Britannica. (2025, January 1). Olympias. *In Encyclopedia Britannica.* https://www.britannica.com/biography/Olympias

The siege of Tyre (332 BCE). (2002). Livius.org. Retrieved February 11, 2025, from https://www.livius.org/articles/battle/tyre-332-bce/

Thomas, C. G. (1968). Alexander the Great and the Unity of Mankind. *The Classical Journal, 63*(6), 258–260. http://www.jstor.org/stable/3295852

Thucydides. (431 B.C.E./1996). *The Peloponnesian War* (R. Warner, Trans.). Penguin Books. (Original work published 431 B.C.E.)

Van Oppen, B. (2014). The Susa Marriages: A Historiographic Note. *Ancient Society, 44,* 25–41. https://www.researchgate.net/publication/331284622_The_Susa_Marriages_A_Historiographic_Note

Vasiloudis, D. (2024, February 12). *Greco-Buddhist art: a fusion of Eastern and Hellenistic traditions.* The Archaeologist. Retrieved February 13, 2025, from https://www.thearchaeologist.org/blog/5b9r28zhcvblv53rtx235htv21d57m

Volkmann, H. (1998). Antigonus I monophthalmus. In *Encyclopaedia Britannica.* Retrieved February 21, 2025, from https://www.britannica.com/biography/Antigonus-I-Monophthalmus

Walbank, F. (2025). Alexander the Great. In *Encyclopaedia Britannica.* Retrieved February 13, 2025, from https://www.britannica.com/biography/Alexander-the-Great

Wasson, D. (2011). Battle of the Granicus. In *World History Encyclopedia.* Retrieved February 11, 2025, from https://www.worldhistory.org/Battle_of_the_Granicus/

Wasson, D. L. (2014). Battle of Hydaspes. In *World History Encyclopedia.* Retrieved February 13, 2025, from https://www.worldhistory.org/article/660/battle-of-hydaspes/

Wasson, D. (2015). Olympias. In *World History Encyclopedia*. Retrieved February 7, 2025, from https://www.worldhistory.org/Olympias/

Wasson, D. (2016a). Cassander. In *World History Encyclopedia*. Retrieved February 21, 2025, from https://www.worldhistory.org/Cassander/

Wasson, D. (2016b). Wars of the Diadochi. In *World History Encyclopedia*. Retrieved February 21, 2025, from https://www.worldhistory.org/Wars_of_the_Diadoch i/

Wasson, D. (2023). The Army of Alexander the Great. In *World History Encyclopedia*. Retrieved February 11, 2025, from https://www.worldhistory.org/article/676/the-army-of-alexander-the-great/

World History Edu. (2024, November 15). *What was the Argead Dynasty?* https://worldhistoryedu.com/what-was-the-argead-dynasty/

Wu, Y. (2022). The relationship between Aristotle and Alexander the Great. *Advances in Social Science, Education and Humanities Research, volume 638*, 71–75. Retrieved February 7, 2025, from https://www.atlantis-press.com/article/125969569.pdf

Zhou, A. (2023, June 19). *The Son of RA: Alexander at Memphis*. The 1440 Review. Retrieved February 13, 2025, from https://1440review.com/2023/06/19/the-son-of-ra-alexander-at-memphis/

Image References

Avantiputra7. (2024, November 25). *The Hellenistic world in 281 BC*. Wikimedia Commons. https://commons.wikimedia.org/wiki/File:Seleucid_Empire_alternative_map_edited.jpg. Licensed under copyright by CC BY-SA 4.0.

Brandmeister~commonswiki. (2014, September 1). *Alexander Mosaic (detail)*. Wikimedia Commons. https://en.wikipedia.org/wiki/File:Alexander_the_Great_mosaic.jpg. Original ca. 120-100 B.C. Public Domain.

Classical Numismatic Group. (2022, April 19). *Coin of Antialkidas*. Wikimedia Commons. https://commons.wikimedia.org/wiki/File:Coin_of_Antialkidas.jpg. Licensed under copyright by CC BY-SA 3.0. Organization website: https://www.cngcoins.com/.

CNG Coins. (2017, June 20). *Philip III Arrhidaios Babylon mint struck under Perdikkas circa 323-320 BC*. Wikimedia Commons. https://commons.wikimedia.org/wiki/File:Philip_III_Arrhidaios_Babylon_mint_struck_under_Perdikkas_circa_323_320_BC.jpg. Licensed under copyright by CC BY-SA 2.5.

Ginolerhino. (2006, July 8). *The Lighthouse of Alexandria on coins minted in Alexandria in the 2nd century*. Wikimedia Commons. https://commons.wikimedia.org/wiki/File:PhareAlexandrie.jpg. Licensed under copyright by CC BY-SA 3.0.

Gun, T. (2010, February 27). Portrait of Niccolò Machiavelli by Santi di Tito. Wikimedia Commons. https://commons.wikimedia.org/wiki/File:Portrait_of_Niccol%C3%B2_Machiavelli_by_Santi_di_Tito.jpg. Public Domain.

Jastrow. (2006). *Aristotle*. Wikimedia Commons. https://commons.wikimedia.org/wiki/File:Aristotle_Altemps_Inv8575.jpg. Public domain.

Le Brun, C. (2019, January 19). *Spithridates attacking Alexander from behind at the Battle of Granicus.* Wikimedia Commons. https://commons.wikimedia.org/wiki/File:Spithridates_attacking_Alexander_from_behind_at_the_Battle_of_Granicus.jpg. Public domain. Detail from *Le Passage du Granique*, 1655.

Martini, F. & The Department of History, United States Military Academy. (2005, June 27). *The Battle of Gaugamela, Alexander's decisive movement, 331 B.C.* Wikimedia Commons. https://commons.wikimedia.org/wiki/File:Battle_gaugamela_decisive.png. Licensed under copyright by CC BY-SA 3.0.

Martini, F. & Department of History, United States Military Academy. (2006, February 24). *Battle of the Hydaspes, Alexander's Crossing.* Wikimedia Commons. https://commons.wikimedia.org/wiki/File:Battle_hydaspes_crossing.png. Public Domain.

Meniashvili, U. (2013, June 8). *Dying Alexander.* Wikimedia Commons. https://commons.wikimedia.org/wiki/File:Dying_Alexander.jpg. Licensed under copyright by CC BY-SA 3.0.

Mortel, R. (2017, June 30). *Phillip II, King of Macedonia, Roman Copy of Greek Original, NY Carlsberg Glyptotek, Copenhagen.* Wikimedia Commons. https://commons.wikimedia.org/wiki/File:Phillip_II,_king_of_Macedonia,_Roman_copy_of_Greek_original,_Ny_Carlsberg_Glyptotek,_Copenhagen_(36420294055).jpg. Licensed under copyright by CC BY 2.0.

Nefasdicere. (2006, August 19). *Thebes.* Wikimedia Commons. https://commons.wikimedia.org/wiki/File:Thebes-1.jpg. Licensed under copyright by CC BY-SA 3.0.

Neilwiththedeal. (2006, October 5). *Alexander and Hephaestion.* Wikimedia Commons. https://commons.wikimedia.org/wiki/File:Alexander_and_Hephaestion.jpg. Public Domain.

Nguyen, M.-L. (2017, July 14). *Alexander the Great NY Carlsberg Glyptotek, Copenhagen.* Wikimedia

Commons. https://commons.wikimedia.org/wiki/File:Alexander_the_Great_Ny_Carlsberg_Glyptotek_IN574_n1.jpg. Licensed under copyright by CC BY 4.0.

PictureObelix. (2013, April 16). *Alexander und Olympias*. Wikimedia Commons. https://commons.wikimedia.org/wiki/File:Alexander_und_Olympias-IMG_5209.JPG. Licensed under copyright by CC BY-SA 3.0 AT.

Raddato, C. (2014, July 4). *Alexander Mosaic (detail)*. Wikimedia Commons. https://commons.wikimedia.org/wiki/File:Darius_III_mosaic.jpg. Licensed under copyright by CC BY-SA 2.0.

Stella. (2019, May 8). *Ptolemy I as Pharaoh of Egypt*. Wikimedia Commons. https://commons.wikimedia.org/wiki/File:Ptolemy_I_as_Pharaoh_of_Egypt.jpg. Licensed under copyright by CC BY-SA 4.0.

The Department of History, United States Military Academy. (2006, March 9). *Battle of Gaugamela, 331 BC - Opening movements*. Wikimedia Commons. https://commons.wikimedia.org/wiki/File:Battle_of_Gaugamela,_331_BC_-_Opening_movements.png. Public Domain.

Unger, R. (2001, February 13). *Temple of Amun, view to the north, Aghurmi, Siwa, Egypt*. Wikimedia Commons. https://commons.wikimedia.org/wiki/File:SiwaAghurmiTemple.jpg. Licensed under copyright by CC BY-SA 3.0.

World Imaging. (2004). *Standing Buddha*. Wikimedia Commons. https://commons.wikimedia.org/wiki/File:Gandhara_Buddha_(tnm).jpeg. Public Domain.

World Imaging. (2006, October 2). *Alexander Cameo*. Wikimedia Commons. https://commons.wikimedia.org/wiki/File:Alexander_Cameo.JPG. Licensed under copyright by CC BY-SA 2.5.

Zifan, A. (2015, October 24). *Achaemenid Empire under different kings (flat map)*. Wikimedia Commons.